CAST *out*
DEMONS

& Slay Your Giants

Other Books by Işık Abla

Be Happy and Free Today!

My Supernatural Encounter

CAST *out* DEMONS

& Slay Your Giants

DISARM AND DEFEAT THE DEMONIC POWERS THAT HINDER YOUR BREAKTHROUGH

IŞIK ABLA

DESTINY IMAGE® PUBLISHERS, INC.
P.O. Box 310, Shippensburg, PA 17257-0310
"Promoting Inspired Lives."

This book and all other Destiny Image and Destiny Image Fiction books are available at Christian bookstores and distributors worldwide.

Cover design by Eileen Rockwell

For more information on foreign distributors, call 717-532-3040.

Reach us on the Internet: www.destinyimage.com.

ISBN 13 TP: 978-0-7684-5374-4

ISBN 13 eBook: 978-0-7684-5375-1

ISBN 13 HC: 978-0-7684-5377-5

ISBN 13 LP: 978-0-7684-5376-8

For Worldwide Distribution, Printed in the U.S.A.

1 2 3 4 5 6 7 8 / 24 23 22 21 20

DEDICATION

First, I would like to thank Jesus for His authorship in my life and ministry. I would like to thank my daughter and husband for their sacrificial support and unconditional love. I would also like to thank Kathleen for her incredible help, patience, and for using her expertise to see that my books are published. Very grateful for you, Kathleen.

You can deliver yourself and others from demonic powers by following the biblical principles in this book.

CONTENTS

Chapter 1

MY PERSONAL TESTIMONY *of* SELF-DELIVERANCE

Today in the Body of Christ, most of God's people ignore the existence and influence of demonic powers. This is exactly what the devil wants, and it is also not scriptural. Because of ignorance, lack of biblical education, and fear of the subject, many people live with demonic bondages most of their lives.

Talking and studying about the devil is almost a taboo subject in the church, yet it was one of the main ministries of our Lord Jesus during His earthly ministry and was part of the ministry of His disciples. We, as the church, have swept it under the carpet and pretended as though the demonic realm doesn't exist. It is backfiring on us.

I tend to agree that we shouldn't give the enemy a center place in our churches or too much attention, which he is always seeking. However, church leaders and ministers have failed to address the subject at all and to help people become free. In large part, the subject has been hushed and has not been addressed biblically by church leaders.

Jesus said, "Follow Me." We as the church haven't been following His example, and every day many captives are walking into our churches in chains, craving the joy, peace, and freedom in Christ. People want their life back and don't know how to get it.

I came to a point of desperation and decided to perform a self-deliverance in my own life because I had no one around to do it. I saw such fear in the ministers and counselors when I spoke about deliverance. I was convinced that if I wanted complete freedom in Christ, it had to happen between Him and me. I had no doubt that He would set me free, because He came to set the captives free. I took Him at His Word.

Coming from Islam, worshiping a false god, mentored by an Islamic scholar great-grandmother (who also operated as a witch doctor), having been molested, abused, and beaten up, and having participated in witchcraft myself, I knew I needed deliverance. I was desperate. I knew that some things were not right, and had to get to the bottom of it.

I got prepared by reading Scriptures and the steps I will be sharing with you later. After spending a good amount of time studying the Word about how Jesus handled the subject and reading many testimonies of deliverance, I went on my knees before my Lord, my Savior and Deliverer, and cast out 48 demons from myself in one night. I was completely and utterly free. I could not put into words the joy and peace that entered my life. During the following months and years, I learned to do self-deliverance whenever I felt it was needed. My freedom in Christ brought freedom in the lives of many, including my husband and friends. I cannot describe the joy I have when people come to tell me how radical a change they've experienced in their lives after following the steps I am sharing in this little book. You can be free today. You can be free and happy. All you need to do is to be desperate enough to take your life back from the enemy, in Jesus' Name.

Powerful Tips

- ✤ *A house divided within itself cannot stand.*
- ✤ *Unity with Jesus Christ is your physical, spiritual, and emotional immunity.*
- ✤ *Unity is your marriage's immunity.*
- ✤ *Unity is your church's immunity.*
- ✤ *Where there is strife and division, there is pride (see Prov. 13:10).*

Chapter 2

A FIRST LOOK *at* DELIVERANCE MINISTRY

I am going to kill someone!" a lady screamed at one of my conferences. She threw herself at the altar and started talking with a man's voice. We took her to the prayer room to do deliverance. It was hard to find even a handful of people to pray with me. After a while, with a few people in attendance with me, I started praying deliverance over her and commanding evil spirits to leave. There was no result. I kept pressing on and there was nothing. Deliverance shouldn't be difficult. If the person is desperate, honest, and wanting Christ's freedom, deliverance is easy, because it is God's will for people to live in freedom, not under the bondage of demons.

When I feel like I am going nowhere in a deliverance session, I usually stop and pray this prayer: "Dear Lord Jesus, please reveal to me through your Holy Spirit, Spirit of Truth, what is preventing this person's freedom. Reveal and remove any hindrances—in Your Name, Jesus, I pray. Amen." I wait quietly after I pray this prayer to hear from the Lord. It usually doesn't take long for God to answer. Sometimes if the answer doesn't come, I bind any interference of the enemy and release the Holy Spirit's truth. And I always receive an answer. God is faithful.

In this situation, when I couldn't get any results, I stopped and sought the Holy Spirit's guidance, and this is what I heard Him say: "This woman was offered as a sexual sacrifice by her uncle, who was a Satanist, when she was three years old. She was molested by many people there at a Satanic ritual. She was forced to drink human blood. She remembers it. But this is not the reason she is not being delivered. She believes in the lie that there is no hope for her. She believes that the drinking of human blood and having been part of a Satanist meeting disqualifies her from salvation and freedom in Christ. You need to cast out the demons of lies and deception from her first."

When I told her what the Holy Spirit told me about her drinking human blood and being offered as a sexual sacrifice, she went into violent convulsions. The devil hates to be exposed. I bound the demons of lies and deception, in Jesus' Name, from speaking the lie to her that she had gone too far to be forgiven. I told her that she had to repent from believing in lies about God's unconditional love and forgiveness. She did. As soon as she repented from believing lies and deception, the rest was easy.

There is *no impossible or hopeless case* for God. As long as you are breathing, there is hope in Christ.

Later on, I witnessed many people receive their freedom once they had been delivered from the demons of lies and deception.

Do You Need Freedom and Deliverance?

Not every case is this dramatic. You may be under demonic bondage and not know how to fight against it. There is an unseen world/dimension that can very much influence and control our well-being without us noticing it most of the time. These bondages cause us to be stuck in the same place, and they prevent us from reaching our full potential. They are basically chains that hinder our spiritual growth and keep us from living the healthy, happy life God intended us to have. With an invisible chain and ball, it is impossible to achieve success and a blessed life. It's time to consider that there may be areas in your life and personality that the enemy has a hold of and is trying to limit you or stop you from going any further. Consider the following symptoms, and if any apply to you, you may be in need of deliverance. Now is the time for you to seek the freedom and deliverance that only Jesus Christ offers and ensures.

- Have you been feeling depressed for some time, with no joy or interest in life, or are you experiencing depression and having suicidal thoughts?

- Are you making impulsive and irrational decisions and always finding yourself in the same mess?

- Do you feel that every day has many challenges that are overwhelming to you, and you're dreading to start the day in the morning?

- Is there a sin in your life that you know is a sin, but it seems like you cannot quit doing it?

- Are you feeling tired and unhappy, and is your heart continuously heavy?

- Are you feeling like you've been stuck in the same place over the years, with the same struggles, and haven't been making the progress in your life you were hoping for?

- Are you living in fear? Anxiety? Panic attacks? Are you having constant breathing problems related to anxiety?

- Are you making the same mistakes over and over, with decisions that result in disaster?

- Do you have strongholds and bondages that are in power in your life?

- Are you feeling a dark presence in your house, your room, or your daily life?

- Are you hearing voices?

- Are you always in a panic mode?

- Are you having constant evil and perverse thoughts and horrific imaginations?

- Have you been under a demonic attack in any form, including nightmares at night?

- Do you have continuous random accidents, early deaths in the family, constant sicknesses, and especially sicknesses that doctors are unable to find the cause for? (Please understand that I am not referring to every sickness as having a demonic or spiritual cause, but many repetitive, undiagnosed, or incurable diseases may be attributed to a demonic cause.)

- Are you always angry or full of rage and bitterness in your heart? (You may not necessarily be showing it on the outside, but is there a storm going on inside?)

- Are you relationally handicapped, losing friends and choosing wrong friends, or getting yourself into troubled and unhealthy relationships that end because of abuse, hurt, and turmoil?

- Have dysfunction, chaos, and turmoil become normal for you and part of your life?

- Are you addicted to certain behaviors or unhealthy habits, including a thinking pattern that is inviting spiritual dark forces?

Never magnify demons, no matter how violent the manifestation may be. Whenever I meet a demon-possessed person who magnifies her or his demons, that is the biggest hindrance. Usually those are the ones who participated in occult practices or sold their souls to the devil through a satanic ritual. Somehow the enemy made them believe he is too powerful to be cast out. That is the biggest lie. There is hope for everyone and every case. No matter how far and deep into the darkness of the demonic they have ventured, Jesus Christ can set them free.

Powerful Tips

- ❖ *Ignorance of demons is demonic. That is exactly what the devil wants—to be invisible. If we pretend he doesn't exist, we allow him to grow stronger.*
- ❖ *Intellectualism in the church promotes ignoring the presence of the enemy, which is a deception from the devil.*
- ❖ *Never magnify demons.*

Is Self-Deliverance Possible?

Yes! And it is a very big *yes!* It wouldn't be the desire of a loving God that you should search the entire country or the planet to find someone to deliver you. He is a loving and merciful God, and Jesus died on the cross for your freedom. When I found no deliverance minister to help me, Jesus said to me, "Come to Me boldly and directly." Please don't misunderstand me—I am not against you going to a deliverance minister to seek help for your deliverance. But I want to emphasize that if you are serious and desperate for your freedom, you don't need a middle man. Jesus is willing and available to help you directly because it is God's will for you to be free. It is His will for you to not live under the dominion of the devil. So when you go to Jesus for your deliverance, you are acting exactly according to His will. Knowing that, have confidence and persevere in faith.

Let us then approach God's throne of grace with confidence, so that we may receive mercy and find grace to help us in our time of need (Hebrews 4:16).

Therefore, brothers and sisters, since we have confidence to enter the Most Holy Place by the blood of Jesus (Hebrews 10:19).

So do not throw away your confidence; it will be richly rewarded (Hebrews 10:35).

Now faith is confidence in what we hope for and assurance about what we do not see (Hebrews 11:1).

This is the confidence we have in approaching God: that if we ask anything according to his will, he hears us (1 John 5:14).

Good news! God wants to set you free! It is *His will* for you to be delivered from the power of the devil.

It is for freedom that Christ has set us free. Stand firm, then, and do not let yourselves be burdened again by a yoke of slavery (Galatians 5:1).

Then they cried to the Lord in their trouble, and he saved them from their distress. He brought them out of darkness, the utter darkness, and broke away their chains. Let them give thanks to the Lord for his unfailing love and his wonderful deeds for mankind, for he breaks down gates of bronze and cuts through bars of iron (Psalm 107:13-16).

So, when you pray for deliverance, know that you are praying according to God's will and He is on your side. Jesus died on the cross for your freedom. You have authority in Jesus Christ!

In him we have redemption through his blood, the forgiveness of sins, in accordance with the riches of God's grace (Ephesians 1:7).

And these signs will accompany those who believe: In my name they will drive out demons; they will speak in new tongues; they will pick up snakes with their hands; and when they drink deadly poison, it will not hurt them at all; they will place their hands on sick people, and they will get well (Mark 16:17-18).

My personal belief is that self-deliverance is more effective, lasting, and powerful than if someone else is doing the deliverance. Why? Because you are taking the full initiative in complete desperation, sincerity, and faith to ask and trust God to set you free. This is more powerful than relying on someone else's faith and performance. Over the years, many passive individuals have asked my help for deliverance, but then neglected and ignored their own part; either they were not delivered, or after a while they lost their freedom because they relied only on my faith and anointing.

However, those I've guided and taught how to be delivered, who themselves did the work, received their freedom and remained free. And let's face it, some individuals only want attention or a quick fix without doing their part. Many don't even want deliverance, even though they say they do. It is difficult to understand, but some people prefer to live with their demons because of their disillusionment and pride. And the enemy tries to use those people to steal my time away from God, from my family, and from the calling God has on my life.

Powerful Tips

❧ *I have seen people demonized through horror, thriller, and vampire movies, and by listening to certain demonic music.*

When you watch, read, or listen to something, you leave your soul wide open to the spirit behind it.

✤ *You are the landlord of your being. You have an authority over yourself. You can evict demons from yourself. But you must mean business. You cannot be passive in deliverance. You must be strong and full of faith.*

Are You Called to a Deliverance Ministry?

I am sharing this with you in case you are interested in a deliverance ministry. You need to know that the moment you enter into this kind of ministry, the devil will do everything in his power to attack you and devastate you. You need to pray for an increase of discernment, for boundaries, and for a strong prayer life. You need to walk in obedience to the Word of God and follow the Holy Spirit's leading. You need a pure life, hiding nothing in the dark. Everything in your life has to be in the light. You must walk a righteous life before the Lord Jesus. The devil knows your weaknesses and your dark secrets, if you have any. Without doing some housecleaning, both figuratively and literally, I don't recommend that you start dealing with the demonic realm. This is especially true if you have any fears. You must deal with your fears and get rid of them immediately, because demons operate mostly through fear.

Some Jews who went around driving out evil spirits tried to invoke the name of the Lord Jesus over those who were demon-possessed. They would say, "In the name of the Jesus whom Paul preaches, I command you to come out." Seven sons of Sceva, a Jewish chief priest, were doing this. One day the evil spirit answered them, "Jesus I know, and Paul I know about, but who are you?" Then the man who had the evil spirit jumped on them

and overpowered them all. He gave them such a beating that
they ran out of the house naked and bleeding (Acts 19:13-16).

I know a young lady who was performing deliverance on many levels and got seriously hurt by demonic forces. She was not living a godly life that was pleasing to the Lord. At the end, she was under more demonic bondages than the people she tried to set free. Because she didn't take living a holy life seriously, she went through turmoil and many sufferings and hurt people, including herself.

A deliverance ministry is not a game or just something very interesting to do because not many are doing it. If you are called to this ministry, that is wonderful, because there is such great need for it. But please reevaluate your life and your walk with Christ very carefully beforehand, using sober judgment. Seek the Holy Spirit's truths to see if there are any open doors in your life. After closing the doors that were opened to the enemy in your life and making it right with God, study the Word of God and establish a strong prayer and devotional life. I truly hope this booklet will be of some help to you in exercising your authority in Christ to cast out devils.

Powerful Tips

❖ *One of the biggest open doors to the demonic is pride. It is the most attractive sin to the devil, because it is his characteristic. The voice that is telling you that you don't need deliverance very well may be the voice of the devil.*

❖ *Pride is blinding.*

❖ *Pride causes denial.*

❖ *Pride is comfortable.*

✤ *The enemy knows how to speak to your pride. He is fluent in pride. He knows how to make you feel right when you are wrong. He knows how to throw blame games and accuse others, instead of taking responsibility for your own actions.*

✤ *Pride is the devil's platform to rule your mind.*

Chapter 3

DEMONS & CHRISTIANS

Laura's father abandoned her along with two siblings and their mother when they were very little. Her mother had to work two jobs to take care of them, and due to her long work hours Laura and her siblings grew up with neither parent being around. She started developing intense self-hatred because of the abandonment and rejection she experienced when she was little. Self-hatred and her termination of unwanted pregnancies opened the doors to the spirits of death and suicide. Desperate for love, she turned to wrong relationships and looked for affection in people who used and abused her. Seeking to find answers to her pain, she turned to New Age, which gave place to a strong demonic residence in her.

When I met her, she was possessed by a legion of demons and was living in constant fear and anxiety. She was a professing Christian at that time. However, she mainly just had much head knowledge. She insisted she was hearing from the Holy Spirit, yet she was hearing from familiar spirits, which is very common in people who practice New Age and spiritualism. Our first deliverance session looked successful, but I knew very strongly that we had only touched the branches and not the main root of the major demonic strongman. She had so many fears and was extremely scared of talking about demons. This is very common with people who are demon-possessed. This kind of fear opens a door to another type of demons—tormenting spirits.

She came to me in desperation a second time after hearing my teaching on incomplete deliverances, which is a very dangerous condition to be in when dealing with possession. Of course, lies and deception play a huge role in this. People who are possessed have serious demonic lies rooted in them. They make up their own truth. What is the sign of incomplete deliverance? Constant fear! What is one of the reasons of incomplete deliverance? Pride that holds back secrets.

Sometimes I sound or look harsh when ministering to an individual in this state, but I have to be truthful. When I told Laura she needed further freedom in certain areas, she was greatly offended and hurt. However, later on she reached out to me, confirming the signs that she needed deliverance. "Then you will know the truth, and the truth will set you free" (John 8:32). When an individual is honest and desperate, the rest is easy through the powerful touch of our wonderful Savior, Jesus. After many confessions of deep, dark secrets, Laura got gloriously delivered from an army of demons and got her life back.

What Are Demons?

Demons are fallen angels who followed Satan and rebelled with him against God. They are evil, impure spirits, and because they have no physical bodies they can operate more effectively in using and influencing people.

Demons are evil spirits. I call demons lie whisperers. If they can inject a negative thought or poison into your mind, they are in your system. They are in. This is why we need to take every thought captive.

The word *spirit* comes from the Greek word *pneuma* and means breath or wind. (The sickness pneumonia also comes from the root word *pneuma*.) This is why many people start yawning heavily during deliverance. These evil spirits, in other words demons, defile people. Defilement means pollution, violation, molestation, and rape, as mentioned in Leviticus 19:31:

> *Give no regard to mediums and familiar spirits; do not seek after them, to be defiled by them: I am the Lord your God* (NKJV).

The enemy begins by controlling people's minds, then over time blends into their personality.

> *And the great dragon was thrown down, that ancient serpent, who is called the devil and Satan, the deceiver of the whole world—he was thrown down to the earth, and his angels were thrown down with him* (Revelation 12:9 ESV).

> *And he said to them, "I saw Satan fall like lightning from heaven"* (Luke 10:18 ESV).

> *And a great sign appeared in heaven: a woman clothed with the sun, with the moon under her feet, and on her head a crown of twelve stars* (Revelation 12:1 ESV).

> *How you are fallen from heaven, O Day Star, son of Dawn! How you are cut down to the ground, you who laid the nations low! You said in your heart, "I will ascend to heaven; above the stars of God I will set my throne on high; I will sit on the mount of assembly in the far reaches of the north; I will ascend above the heights of the clouds; I will make myself like the Most High." But you are brought down to Sheol, to the far reaches of the pit* (Isaiah 14:12-15 ESV).

Demon Possessed or Oppressed?

There is only one word for demonic indwelling; it is the word *daimonizomai*, which in Greek means "demonized, having demons."

Through many experiences I have learned that God's people can be under the oppression of a demonic power that can even lead to possession if they choose to entertain and encounter evil. This is a very sensitive subject that goes all the way to the questions: "Can a person lose their salvation?" or, "Could it be that the person was not saved to begin with?" I am not interested in getting into this debate in any fashion, but my personal experiences with demonized people, even in the church, caused me to ask those questions.

We see the first mention of a demon in the Scriptures in First Samuel 16:14:

> *Now the Spirit of the Lord had departed from Saul, and an evil spirit from the Lord tormented him.*

I just need to interject here that the evil spirit was not *from* the Lord, but was with His permission, just as in the Book of Job God gave permission for Satan to test Job.

Powerful Tips

* *The devil can speak to you in your first-person voice. When you say terrible things about yourself, he is the one feeding your mind with his whispers.*
* *Faith comes through hearing. Watch what you hear about yourself, others, and about God.*
* *Anything that's controlling you and you can't stop its control has power over you. That is your bondage. That's your chain. You can break that chain through deliverance in Jesus Christ.*

Can a Christian Be Demon Possessed?

I have to answer this question in several ways. There are four different types of demonic activity we might encounter as Christians.

True Confession of Faith

Can a Christian be demon possessed? No. However, I have seen demonic manifestations that were extremely violent and radical, which made me question whether the saving knowledge of Christ was true in the person's life. I have done deliverance on individuals who grew up in Christian homes and professed to be Christian, but never had a personal relationship with Jesus or heard from the Holy Spirit. In nearly every deliverance, I asked for the person's confession of faith declaring Jesus Christ as their Lord and Savior. There were some individuals who couldn't declare their faith, because the moment they tried demonic manifestations took place. There are many signs and symptoms whereby the Holy Spirit reveals truth. I believe we need to study each case separately.

Once, a young girl who was a pastor's daughter, and had grown up in a Christian home, manifested the spirit of Python. She later confessed that she was living on her parents' faith and didn't know Christ. Whenever believers praised or prayed in tongues, she would get extremely uneasy, and finally at a powerful prayer meeting she manifested many demons.

Under the Influence

A saved person can also be very much under the influence of demonic powers by just being under the influence of alcohol. If there is a weakness and/or an open door in that person's life, demonic influences can be as devastating as possession. For example, there are many Christians who live such worldly lifestyles that their moral standards are very much conformed to the world's values instead of God's. I would suggest that is a very dangerous place to be and live.

The Bible says that friendship with the world is being an enemy toward God (see James 4:4). Who is the enemy of God? The devil. I believe the moment anyone begins conforming to the ways of the world, that person is opening a wide door to demonic forces, whether you call it possession or oppression.

Hearing from the Devil

A Christian can hear from the devil. One of the biggest deceptions in the Body of Christ today is that Christians only hear from the Holy Spirit. What a lie!

In Matthew 16, Jesus asked a very important question: "Who do you say that I am?" Peter, as usual, jumped in and answered. He said, "You are the Messiah, the Son of the living God."

Jesus was well pleased with his answer and said, "Blessed are you Simon, son of Jonah. This was not revealed to you by man, but by My Father in Heaven." Wow! This is a very powerful statement coming from our Lord Jesus. He is confirming that Peter received a revelation directly from the Father. That is incredible. Peter heard the voice of God.

Yet in the same chapter, a little further down, Peter started rebuking Jesus after hearing He was going to suffer and die. Right in the same chapter, after being praised by the Lord for hearing from the Father, Peter was rebuked and, moreover, was called "Satan" as Jesus said, "Get behind Me, Satan!"

Was Peter Satan? Of course not. But he was the mouthpiece of Satan. It can be reasoned that Jesus was speaking directly to the demon who had influenced Peter to speak against the will of God.

In the same way, a believer in Christ who confesses that Christ is the Messiah and Lord can hear from the enemy. And the moment you hear from the devil, if you don't keep your thoughts captive, you allow the enemy to enter in through your thought pattern.

> *We demolish arguments and every pretension that sets itself up against the knowledge of God, and we take captive every thought to make it obedient to Christ* (2 Corinthians 10:5).

There are many Christians who are believing the lies of the enemy about themselves, others, their lives, and even God. Believing in the lies of the devil is empowering him in your life.

When the enemy tells you a lie, you must ask, "What is my heavenly Father saying about this?"

During my meetings and conferences, many people were set free from demonic bondages just by confessing, renouncing, and repenting from the lies they believed. They repented from making a pact/agreement with the enemy by believing him rather than believing God.

Demonic Bondage

Christians can have demonic bondages. While we argue about possession and oppression, many believers live their lives in depression, with suicidal thoughts, without joy, having addictions such as pornography and violent movies (including vampire movie addictions), which deliberately open many doors to the enemy.

Demonic manifestations that are radical and violent are the easier ones to recognize. But the most concerning part is that sometimes the demonic is so blended into the person's character and actions that it is not easily recognizable. There are many Jezebels, Ahabs, Judases, Absaloms, and even Antichrists I encounter in the ministry, sometimes daily. Are these all possessed or oppressed? Who cares? What is important is that they are under the influence and control of the devil and are as damaging as any beast could be to the Body of Christ. This is all you need to know.

The point is, even without being *possessed*, a Christian can be tormented and affected by demonic activity in various ways. All of it is demonic, and all of it is inferior to the power of the blood of Jesus Christ. We have authority over the demonic through His shed blood, and there is no good reason, ever, to tolerate or live with any form of demonization. Cast it out!

Powerful Tips

✤ *Serpents like to hide in the dark. They are quiet. In the same way, demons usually enter through people's blind sides. They are in the familiar, so they can't be noticed. The very behavior pattern you are defending may very well be where the serpent is hiding.*

✤ *People get stuck unless their secret serpents are revealed. Once it is brought to the light and cast out, they are free to fulfill their full potential. Serpents hinder.*

Chapter 4

WHAT *is* WARFARE?

Warfare is a demonic spiritual attack. It is a spiritual battle between the children of God and the dark forces of the devil. The moment you are pressured, stressed, depressed, feeling discouraged, empty, hateful, having a short fuse, or negative, lustful, angry, or bitter thoughts are flooding your mind, you are under a spiritual attack called warfare. It is almost ridiculous how many churches accept that there is something called "warfare" but deny that it is demonic. It is almost considered a natural mood swing without talking about the source of it. Warfare is a pure demonic attack. Yes, it can most definitely affect your mood swings and feelings too.

Warfare is engaging a different dimension. It's not happening in your dimension. You can feel it, but you may not see it. The demonic is trying to hurt you, and many times they're doing this by using people. For you to fight against something, you need to know your enemy. Your enemy is not people, "flesh and blood," but the devil's army.

Because warfare is a supernatural attack, you cannot win your battles in the flesh. You have to submit to the Holy Spirit and take up your divine weapon.

> *The weapons we fight with are not the weapons of the world. On the contrary, they have divine power to demolish strongholds* (2 Corinthians 10:4).

The moment you find yourself asking, "Why am I feeling this way? What is the matter with me?"—you are under a spiritual attack. It is warfare, and it is demonic.

It is very saddening that God's people have so little knowledge about warfare and don't know how to fight against it. Therefore, the warfare begins turning into depression and suicide, all because the enemy is hunting God's people who are off guard.

> *Put on the full armor of God, so that you can take your stand against the **devil's schemes**. For our struggle is not against flesh and blood, **but against the rulers, against the authorities, against the powers of this dark world and against the spiritual forces of evil in the heavenly realms**. Therefore put on the full armor of God, so that when the day of evil comes, you may be able to stand your ground, and after you have done everything, to stand. Stand firm then, with the belt of truth buckled around your waist, with the breastplate of righteousness in place, and with your feet fitted with the readiness that comes from the gospel of peace. In addition to all this, take up the shield of faith, with which you can extinguish all the **flaming arrows of the evil one**. Take the helmet of salvation and the **sword of the Spirit**, which is the word of God* (Ephesians 6:11-17).

I am only going to reflect on the bolded parts of this powerful portion of Scripture.

1. **The devil schemes** against you. He makes plans, has a will, and designs assignments to harm you.

2. **There is a fight/struggle**—other translations say a "wrestling" or a "battle." We are wrestling with the supernatural. Can you

grasp how serious this fight is? And in most churches we are not taught how to fight.

3. **Our fight or problem is not with people.** Our enemy is the devil and his army. And just like in an army, they have ranks, titles, and assignments. Demons are not just going around looking for anyone coming their way. They have an assignment and a plan against you and your loved ones. This is crucial for you to understand in order to defeat the enemy and kick him out of your life.

    i. There are spirits, which are demons, controlling and influencing people to do the things they do against us to devastate us. Once you know which principality is ruling over that person, you can bind that spirit and make it ineffective. I will be sharing more about binding and loosing based on the Word of God. It is very important to know how to bind any spirit against you, against your family, children, neighborhood, work, and even your country.

4. Because of this, **you need to put on the full armor of God.** It is not optional. It is mandatory, because it says *when* the evil comes. Not *if*, but *when*. So each of us, as God's children, will go through warfare. Why? Because it will strengthen us, increase our faith, and draw us nearer to God if we fight the battle—not in the flesh, but in the spirit.

    i. *The battle is spiritual.* Then how can we win a battle that is supernatural? How can our yelling, screaming, planning, and fighting in the flesh make us victorious in a spiritual battle? We cannot win the battle with our human strength or power. Understanding this changed my life and my walk with Christ. It will change yours too if you learn to fight your battles with the supernatural power of God.

5. **Flaming arrows of the evil one!** What are these arrows? They are lies that you believe about yourself, discouraging and negative thoughts, magnified failures, gossip and slander behind your back, accusations and blame games, betrayals, rejections, anger outbursts, nervous breakdowns, uncontrollable crying episodes, numbness, and much more.

6. **You can win this battle with the Sword of the Spirit, which is the Word of God.** God has given you a divine weapon. You take it into your hand, and if you know how to use it, you defeat your supernatural opponent, your vicious enemy, or your Goliath or Jezebel with that weapon. How amazing is that? But are you using it? Are you believing in it? Are you trained and disciplined to use your sword to slay your giants? Maybe the time has come for you to start winning and not losing anymore!

Powerful Tips

✤ *Whatever you are obsessed with is your idol. Whatever you are always thinking of or focused on is your god. That is a wide-open door to the enemy.*

✤ *Praying in tongues confuses and devastates the enemy. People who say they believe in tongues but secretly despise tongues are under the influence of the enemy. Mocking or despising the gift of the Holy Spirit is an offense to God. The devil delights in you when you are against tongues.*

Warfare Prayer Declaration

This prayer must be prayed out loud, because your voice is your weapon. Your voice is your machine gun. You activate your faith when you *declare*.

Dear Lord Jesus,

I praise You, my Lord, and put myself completely under Your authority and surrender to Your will. You are my Lord and Savior, and there is no other. Jesus, You are King of kings and Lord of lords. I declare that You have also given me authority. I cover myself, my family, my children, my ministry, and every work that I do with Your precious and powerful blood right now. I surrender every area of my life, my whole heart, mind, and body to You right now. You are the ultimate authority in my life. I worship You only. You are the center and the ruler of my life. You are worthy to receive all praise, glory, and honor.

I am very grateful for Your sacrifice on the cross to set me free from the power of darkness and eternal condemnation. I am very grateful for You shedding Your blood for me at Calvary. Through the shedding of Your blood, I have redemption. I put all my hope and trust in You. I acknowledge You in all my ways as my only source of strength, joy, peace, wisdom, and deliverance. I receive Your love right now. I receive Your strength right now. I receive all You have for me right now, and I am in agreement with Your intercessory prayer for me. And I say amen to Your will in my life.

I declare and decree victory over my life and the lives of my family and children right now in Your Name, Jesus. I declare and decree that every one of Your promises written in Your Holy Word, which is the sword of the Spirit and is my spiritual weapon, is fulfilled in my life. I declare that I am Your child and belong to You. I declare that I belong to light, and darkness has no place in my life or destiny.

Lord Jesus, I ask You to forgive all my sins. I repent from any unrighteousness. I repent from opening any doors to the enemy. I forgive all people who hurt me and did wrong to me. I hold no bitterness or grudge against anyone. Please, my Lord, search my heart and cleanse me from any bitterness, unforgiveness, and unrighteousness. I bless those who harmed me and persecuted me.

I command every spirit of witchcraft, every curse and assignment of the devil to be destroyed in Your Name, Jesus. I put a blood line of Jesus Christ between me and the enemy, between my family and the enemy. The devil cannot cross that blood boundary line. With the authority my Lord Jesus has given me in His Word, I command the enemy to flee from me. I submit to God and resist the devil. I bind the enemy in Jesus' Name and release the Holy Spirit's power, love, peace, joy, and sound mind. I bind any tormenting, hateful, lying, deceiving, mean, bullying, lustful, and familiar spirits, including the spirits of Jezebel, Python, and Leviathan in Jesus' Name, and I send them to where my Lord Jesus chooses. They have no power over me and my family, in Jesus' Name.

I release supernatural joy, blessings, and strength over my life and family right now. I refuse to believe any lies and negative words spoken into my life or into the lives of my loved ones and my ministry. I believe in God's truth and declare His wonderful plans over my life and over the lives of my loved ones. I am encouraged and empowered by the Word of God to be steadfast and filled with faith. In Jesus' mighty Name, I pray all this. Amen.

Powerful Tips

✤ *Even when you don't know what kind of demonic presence or force it is, you can still cast demons out in Jesus' Name.*

✤ *The devil and his demons are bullies. They operate through fear. You must first cast out the demon of fear to cast them out.*

✤ *I have seen people get delivered from many demons just by shouting out loud, "Jesus Christ is my Lord. Jesus Christ is my Lord. Jesus Christ is my Lord." They stuttered at the beginning. But as they pushed through repeating it, they were set free without my even having to intervene. Our words have power.*

Warfare Scriptures

Praying the following Scriptures will help you tremendously in defeating the enemy, because you are agreeing with God and activating the power of His Word, which is your sword and your supernatural weapon against the devil. Pray and proclaim these Scriptures out loud, day and night, to defeat the prince of the air.

When the enemy comes in like a flood, the Spirit of the Lord will lift up a standard against him (Isaiah 59:19 NKJV).

"No weapon forged against you will prevail, and you will refute every tongue that accuses you. This is the heritage of the servants of the Lord, and this is their vindication from me," declares the Lord (Isaiah 54:17).

Tyranny [oppression, abuse and cruelty] *will be far from you; you will have nothing to fear. Terror will be far removed; it will not come near you* (Isaiah 54:14).

No harm will overtake you, no disaster will come near your tent (Psalm 91:10).

The weapons we fight with are not the weapons of the world. On the contrary, they have divine power to demolish strongholds (2 Corinthians 10:4).

I pray that out of his glorious riches he may strengthen you with power through his Spirit in your inner being (Ephesians 3:16).

So that Christ may dwell in your hearts through faith. And I pray that you, being rooted and established in love (Ephesians 3:17).

In addition to all this, take up the shield of faith, with which you can extinguish all the flaming arrows of the evil one (Ephesians 6:16).

Christ redeemed us from the curse of the law by becoming a curse for us, for it is written: "Cursed is everyone who is hung on a pole" (Galatians 3:13).

Sovereign Lord, my strong deliverer, you shield my head in the day of battle (Psalm 140:7).

He will cover you with his feathers, and under his wings you will find refuge; his faithfulness will be your shield and rampart (Psalm 91:4).

But I will sing of your strength, in the morning I will sing of your love; for you are my fortress, my refuge in times of trouble (Psalm 59:16).

Deliver me from my enemies, O God; be my fortress against those who are attacking me (Psalm 59:1).

You are my refuge and my shield; I have put my hope in your word (Psalm 119:114).

The blood will be a sign for you on the houses where you are, and when I see the blood, I will pass over you. No destructive plague will touch you when I strike Egypt (Exodus 12:13).

They triumphed over him by the blood of the Lamb and by the word of their testimony; they did not love their lives so much as to shrink from death (Revelation 12:11).

Now may the God of peace, who through the blood of the eternal covenant brought back from the dead our Lord Jesus, that great Shepherd of the sheep, equip you with everything good for doing his will, and may he work in us what is pleasing to him, through Jesus Christ, to whom be glory for ever and ever. Amen (Hebrews 13:20-21).

Therefore, brothers and sisters, since we have confidence to enter the Most Holy Place by the blood of Jesus (Hebrews 10:19).

How much more, then, will the blood of Christ, who through the eternal Spirit offered himself unblemished to God, cleanse our consciences from acts that lead to death, so that we may serve the living God! (Hebrews 9:14)

Then I heard a loud voice in heaven say: "Now have come the salvation and the power and the kingdom of our God, and the authority of his Messiah. For the accuser of our brothers and sisters, who accuses them before our God day and night, has been hurled down" (Revelation 12:10).

To Jesus the mediator of a new covenant, and to the sprinkled blood that speaks a better word than the blood of Abel (Hebrews 12:24).

Praise be to the Lord my Rock, who trains my hands for war, my fingers for battle (Psalm 144:1).

You made my enemies turn their backs in flight, and I destroyed my foes (Psalm 18:40).

I have given you authority to trample on snakes and scorpions and to overcome all the power of the enemy; nothing will harm you (Luke 10:19).

You, dear children, are from God and have overcome them, because the one who is in you is greater than the one who is in the world. They are from the world and therefore speak from the viewpoint of the world, and the world listens to them (1 John 4:4-5).

Powerful Tips

❧ *Friendship with the world is being an enemy toward God. The more you become worldly, the more you become an enemy of God. Do the math. If you are an enemy of God, whose friend are you? God is calling us to a holy and consecrated life.*

❧ *Pornography brings sexual demons and generational curses into the household. It affects the entire family. It affects the physical, mental, and financial well-being of everyone in the house. I have seen crippling diseases upon family members when the head of the household was addicted to pornography.*

Chapter 5

SOUL WOUNDS

"He restores my soul." —Psalm 23:3 NKJV

Before we go any further into what opens the doors to the demonic, we need to understand that soul wounds are major gateways into the demonic realms. We all have souls. Our souls get hurt through our sins and other people's sins against us. Various traumatic events—such as rape, molestation, witnessing a murder, or suicide in the family, etc.—deeply wound people's souls and open wide doors to complete possession of that soul by demonic forces.

When we talk about a broken heart, we are really talking about a wounded soul.

We are created in God's own image (see Gen. 1:27). As God is a triune being (Trinity, one God in three persons), so are we. We are created in three parts:

1. Soul

2. Spirit

3. Body

Our soul is *ego* in Greek—our mind, will, and emotions. Ego is centered around "I." What I want, I think, I believe, I feel, I like—it is all about me, myself, and I. Ego exalts self—self-centered, selfish, self-promoting, self-advertising. When we say egotistical or egocentric, we are talking about people who are into themselves. We all have a free will, that is, the responsibility of choosing between good or evil, as in Genesis 3:22. Our soul gets bruised and wounded because of our sins and other people's sins committed against us.

> *Whoever commits adultery with a woman lacks understanding; he who does so destroys his own soul* (Proverbs 6:32 NKJV).

> *But he who sins against me wrongs his own soul; all those who hate me love death* (Proverbs 8:36 NKJV).

> *A man shall eat well by the fruit of his mouth, but the soul of the unfaithful feeds on violence* (Proverbs 13:2 NKJV).

> *Take My yoke upon you and learn from Me, for I am gentle and lowly in heart, and you will find rest for your souls* (Matthew 11:29 NKJV).

> *He who disdains instruction despises his own soul, but he who heeds rebuke gets understanding* (Proverbs 15:32 NKJV).

> *And its foundations will be broken. All who make wages will be troubled of soul* (Isaiah 19:10 NKJV).

> *A fool's mouth is his destruction, and his lips are the snare of his soul* (Proverbs 18:7 NKJV).

> *He who has clean hands and a pure heart, who has not lifted up his soul to an idol, nor sworn deceitfully* (Psalm 24:4 NKJV).

> *And my soul shall be joyful in the Lord; it shall rejoice in His salvation* (Psalm 35:9 NKJV).

Why are you cast down, O my soul? And why are you disquieted within me? Hope in God, for I shall yet praise Him for the help of His countenance (Psalm 42:5 NKJV).

My soul melts from heaviness; strengthen me according to Your word (Psalm 119:28 NKJV).

There are major soul wounds that become open doors to demonic influences.

1. Rejected Soul

This happens through *abandonment* and *neglect*. These are major open doors to many demonic forces and other scars in the soul such as trust issues, drama addiction, anger, bitterness, jealousy, covetousness, self-hatred (leads to suicide if it is not dealt with), extreme emotions, high-maintenance, codependency, neediness, people-pleasing, poor self-image, attention-seeking, inferiority complexes, being hard on self, condemning others, blame games, instability, and a lying tongue.

- Ishmael was rejected by his biological father, Abraham, and that caused a soul wound that caused a generational curse of anger and hostility among his descecndants, Muslims.
- King David's daughter, Tamar, was raped by her half-brother Amnon, and she lived as a desolate woman the rest of her life. Incest-rape brought shame and condemnation to the wounding of her soul, which caused her isolation.
- Jezebel, a daughter of a pagan king, was given away in marriage as a piece of property and was a wounded soul because of rejection and abandonment. That deep soul wound opened up a wide door to the demonic.

- King Saul was tormented by a demon because of his soul wound through his sin of disobedience and rebellion. He opened a door to the demonic and was tormented by an evil spirit.

I have met many children adopted by loving families, yet their souls were scarred by the event of their abandonment, and they felt fear and anger from rejection all their lives until their souls got healed.

Many people who were rejected or abandoned during their childhood carry the "orphan spirit." They feel sorry for themselves and compare themselves with others who have loving families, and they feel lonely and worthless. They think, "Something must be wrong with me for my mother or father to abandon or reject me."

Rejected people often go to any length and depth to be accepted and noticed. They carry deep scars until they are healed from their soul wounds.

2. Betrayed Soul

Betrayal results in disappointment, frustration, discouragement, bitterness, rage, hatred, poor self-image, paranoia, and suspicion.

Once someone is betrayed, especially during childhood by parents who were the most responsible to love and protect them, they develop suspicion and paranoia and do not trust anyone. Betrayal at a young age shakes a child to his core. He will carry distrust until his soul is restored. He may have a distorted image of God in his mind and will have a hard time trusting God.

A lady who had been ill for a decade, suffering with thyroid problems and arthritis, got immediately healed just by repenting from her hatred and bitterness toward her boss. She was slandering and spreading rumors about her boss a decade ago because of unfair treatment at the workplace. Her bitterness and hatred started eating her from the inside and eventually opened up a wide door to the demon of infirmity. You need to deal with your negative emotions before they become a gate to the demonic gangs and start hurting your health.

Those who have been betrayed need to reconnect with the Holy Spirit. He is called the Spirit of Truth in John 14:17, John 15:26, and John 16:13. Whenever you don't know what is going on but sense that something is wrong, or you are confused, under attack, or getting nowhere during deliverance, pause and take a moment to pray, "Holy Spirit, Spirit of Truth, please reveal to me what is happening right now, in Jesus' Name I pray, amen." He is going to bring things to light.

Be patient and quiet while waiting for Holy Spirit to reveal His truth to you. It is usually the very first thing that comes to your mind that is your answer. The enemy tries to manipulate afterward.

3. Fearful Soul

Abuse, rape, molestation, etc. open the doors to the spirit of torment, lies, deception, self-hatred, and condemnation. People who suffer from this are always expecting the worst outcome. They develop speech problems, fear of people, fear of death, fear of accidents, and fear of sickness.

Fear plays a huge factor in the wounding of a soul. People who grew up under fear and oppression are open to tormenting spirits. I have prayed over many people who were healed of cancer but lived the rest of their lives in fear of cancer.

I know a young girl who wouldn't go anywhere because of fear of accidents. She believed something terrible was going to happened to her. Because her mother died in a car accident, she believed that she too was prone to accidents. As you can see, believing in a lie also hinders people from getting healed of their soul wounds.

The traumas that cause this fear must be released and forgiven. In several cases, I've seen different health issues such as cancer, and especially many advanced skin diseases, completely healed by forgiveness. Immediate forgiveness brings immediate healing without specifically praying for healing. And I have to mention, self-forgiveness is as important as forgiving others.

4. Lost or Wandering Soul

This type of soul is indecisive, easily influenced and persuaded, double-minded, insecure, a workaholic, lacks commitment, and may be affected by a spirit of divorce, distrust, tiredness, or fatigue. People who carry this soul wound are weary, tired, and frustrated. They usually are prone to the spirit of fatigue and depression. They can't seem to find their place and purpose in life, and they feel lost.

This soul condition is created by an unstable lifestyle and cannot commit or be sure of anything. I had a friend whose father was in the military and had to move all the time. She had a deep soul wound and couldn't make any commitments in friendships, work, church, or even marriage. Moving constantly in childhood hurt her soul, and she saw every relationship as temporary. She was afraid to commit, believing that one day she was going to lose the relationship anyway. She was unstable in all of her relationships until she got healed from her soul wound.

5. Humiliations and Embarrassment

This soul manifests in insecurities, poor self-image, fear of people, fear of failure, isolation, distrust, paranoia, and anger. It is especially people who have been bullied who have this soul wound. They dread to be in public and fear making a fool of themselves when they talk. They hide behind masks and avoid getting close with anyone. They want to be invisible so that no one can pick on them.

Many times as a little girl, I was called names and severely beaten up by teachers in front of my classroom. The entire classroom laughed at me and made fun of me. Many times I was called ugly names by my parents in public. Those events hurt me deeply, and I carried that soul wound for a long time, until I got healed.

6. Wounds of Condemnation

Many people raised under harsh and excessive discipline carry the soul wound of condemnation, which operates with the tormenting spirits of guilt and shame. They are hard on themselves (a form of self-hatred and poor self-image); have a negative thinking pattern; are hard on others (judgmental and critical); and they can be harsh, shameful, guilt-ridden, hostile, cruel, angry, and bitter. Also, this can manifest in a religious spirit and legalism.

Especially in shame-and-guilt-focused cultures like those in the Middle East, people live in shame and guilt all their lives. A girl who gets raped or abused also carries scars of shame and guilt. The spirit of condemnation enters in through this soul wound as do the religious and judgmental spirits. This soul wound is so very deep that the person gets tormented by her every action, judging herself constantly, and being extremely hard on herself as well as on others. She can't live at peace with herself and others until she is healed and restored to her true identity in Christ.

7. Conflicted Soul

This person goes back and forth between spirit and flesh. They are unreliable, highly creative and visionary, indecisive, double-minded, unstable, prideful, overly committed or lacking commitment (two extremes), tormented between ideas and visions.

This damaged soul is in constant conflict. Divorces and family fights are some of the causes, when children are pulled and manipulated by their parents to take sides. Also, when one parent praises the child and another verbally abuses the child, the child enters into an identity crisis and doubts who she is. Generally, children raised by only one parent have this soul wound, but the cause is not limited to that circumstance. I know a woman whose husband left her for another woman. She later married a loving man but couldn't receive his loving words and praises because her soul was in conflict due to the wounds from her previous marriage.

Fear of failure also torments a conflicted soul and keeps it from making decisions in any area of life. It causes a person to be stuck in between places of life due to the inability to make up one's mind.

Be very careful with what you watch, read, and hear. Those are gateways to your soul. I have seen many people wounded by horror/vampire or pornographic movies and hard rock or heavy metal music. I have also met many people who, by listening to eastern religions' music, were heavily under demonic influences, just because they opened the door of their souls to those kinds of entertainments.

Do not receive negative words or predictions for your future. The devil uses people as his mouthpiece to devastate and torment them. Do not make an agreement with lies of others by agreeing and believing in their negative words.

The devil is called the prince of the power of the air. *Air!* This is why you cannot pray deliverance and warfare prayers silently in your heart. You have to be vocal. You have to speak out loud, declaring and proclaiming the Word of God and commanding the enemy to leave in Jesus' Name.

Prayer for Soul Wounds

Dear Lord Jesus,

I declare that You are my Lord and Savior. I believe that You died on the cross for my sins to set me free and heal me. Thank You for Your sacrifice to give me eternal life, healing, and freedom from all hurts and bondages. I declare that because of Your wounds I am healed. And I declare that because of Your wounds and stripes my soul wounds are also healed. I ask You to touch each and every soul wound in me and heal them one by one with Your powerful blood, Jesus. Thank You, Lord Jesus, for healing me and making my heart whole. I receive my healing and freedom in Your matchless name, Jesus Christ. Amen.

What Opens the Door to the Demonic?

Please go through the following list and see if you practice or have been subject to anything listed below:

- Rejection, abandonment, and neglect
- Abuse, molestation, and rape
- Tragic events, loss of a parent or loved one
- Trauma
- Curses—generational curses or any verbal curses
- Magic—white or black magic
- Soul ties, blood pacts, codependency, needy or controlling relationships, vows, covenants (soul mate is not a biblical term and not to be used for anyone)
- Sexual immorality

- Dysfunctional families
- Religious and legalistic families
- Occult practices
- False religions
- Trances
- Medium readings
- Telepathy
- Tarot cards
- Horoscopes
- Palm reading
- Hypnosis
- Mind control/mind power
- New Age practices
- False idols (money, sex, career, power, fame, music, or people, including making idols of your children or parents)
- Yoga (as a religious practice)
- Superstitions
- Christian Science
- Jehovah's Witnesses
- Scientology
- Violent movies and games (horror movies, vampire movies, violent movies, sexual movies, even perverse comedies and games)
- Music—violent, sexual, or seductive content in music
- Pornography
- Spirit guides
- Ouija board
- Out-of-body experiences
- Hare Krishna
- Freemasonry
- Witchcraft, Wicca, and sorcery
- Channeling
- Numerology
- Handwriting reading and analyzing
- Fetishism/charms
- Mormonism
- Unitarianism/Universalism
- Hinduism
- Buddhism
- Bahaism
- Islam
- Other religions

Powerful Renunciations for
Repentance and Cleansing

Death and life are in the power of the tongue (Proverbs 18:21 NKJV).

Many people don't realize how powerful this Scripture is. If death and life are in the power of the tongue, everything in between is in the power of the tongue as well.

With your words either you are empowering God or the devil in your life. Who are your words making an agreement with? Are you putting a curse over yourself, your marriage, your spouse, your children, and your life with your words?

Repent of and renounce every lie and curse that you, others, or the enemy have spoken over your life, or that you have spoken over the lives of others. Break your agreement with the devil's will.

> *I renounce and repent from my ego, arrogance, pride, haughtiness, judgmentalism, harsh criticism of others, disobedience, and rebellion in the Name of Jesus, and I cover myself with the blood of Jesus.*
>
> *I renounce and repent from every ungodly thought and behavior pattern in the Name of Jesus, and I cover myself with the blood of Jesus.*
>
> *I renounce and repent from all violence, rage, hatred, hostility, revenge, abusive behavior, harsh and rude behaviors, bullying, intimidation, resentment, revenge, retaliation, unforgiveness, and bitterness in the Name of Jesus, and I cover myself with the blood of Jesus.*

I renounce and repent from all false religions, occults, witchcraft, sorcery, divination, New Age, involvement in cults, horoscopes, tarot reading, consulting spirits, satanic rituals, blood sacrifices, blood pacts, and all other practices that are against the Word of God in the Name of Jesus, and I cover myself with the blood of Jesus.

I renounce and repent from all lust, perversion, sexual addiction, adultery, pornography, uncleanness, impurity, seduction, fantasies, watching sensual and sexual movies, perverse and coarse joking and speaking, and every sexual sin in the Name of Jesus, and I cover myself with the blood of Jesus.

I renounce and repent from every wrongdoing, all lies, deception, manipulation, exaggeration, and falsehood in the Name of Jesus, and I cover myself with the blood of Jesus.

I renounce and repent from all soul ties through sexual and emotional or spiritual attachments including blood pacts, ungodly covenants, vows, oaths, and all demonic ties through fornication, ungodly friendships and relationships, and even all ungodly soul ties of my ancestors in the Name of Jesus, and I cover myself with the blood of Jesus.

I renounce and repent from all addictions to food, gluttony, alcohol, drugs, shopping, TV, internet, pornography, and any other addiction in the Name of Jesus, and I cover myself with the blood of Jesus.

I renounce and repent from all selfishness, self-centeredness, self-advertising, self-promotion, self-glory seeking, self-hatred, self-pity, self-rejection, and self-disqualification in the Name of Jesus, and I cover myself with the blood of Jesus.

I renounce and repent from all gossip, slander, accusations, blame games, cruel speech, verbal abuse and attacks in the Name of Jesus, and I cover myself with the blood of Jesus.

I renounce and repent from all control, manipulation, victim behavior, self-pity, drama addiction, and attention-seeking in the Name of Jesus, and I cover myself with the blood of Jesus.

I renounce and repent from all fear, worry, anxiety, and from allowing the enemy to torment me in the Name of Jesus, and I cover myself with the blood of Jesus.

I renounce and repent from operating through Jezebel, Python, and Leviathan. I expel them and reject any of their power over my life and soul in the Name of Jesus, and I cover myself with the blood of Jesus.

I renounce guilt, shame, condemnation, and all feelings of dirtiness and filthiness in the Name of Jesus, and I cover myself with the blood of Jesus.

Powerful Tips

❖ *People with a victim mentality, who are usually abused and rejected people, act like the world owes them something, and they push people away with their neediness.*

❖ *Insecure people are high-maintenance people. Whatever you do, you can't make them happy or feel good about themselves.*

❖ *Insecure people get easily offended.*

❖ *Being around an insecure person is like walking on eggshells and is very exhausting.*

✤ *If you are feeling a demonic presence around you or in your household or you are under attack, surround yourself with the Word of God and worship music. Put on an audio Bible 24/7 in your house, your workplace, and your car. The devil cannot stand it and will leave.*

Chapter 6

DEMONIC GROUPS *or* GANGS

A woman from Sweden who was one of my viewers sent me a message that she was watching my program at the mental institution she was in. She said she had spent most of her adult life in and out of the mental clinic and was seeing snakes everywhere. She was terrified and tormented. If they could make her sleep with heavy medication, she would wake up seeing her bed, herself, and the floor covered with snakes. She had to be medicated all the time, but the medication was having serious side effects and her health was declining.

One day, as someone was going through the television channels, she saw my program and begged to be allowed to watch it. Then she heard me speaking about deliverance from the demonic. I just want to interject an important point here—in my experience in the ministry, I have learned that the Holy Spirit can still reach a person's conscience if there is an open door in that person's heart, even though they may be intoxicated with drugs or alcohol.

This woman told me I was her only hope, to which I replied that her only hope was Jesus and that I was only going to facilitate. She was a desperate and willing individual. I called her and we started the process to her freedom over the phone. Every call she started doing better and better. She started seeing the snakes less and less. This took place in a deliverance session every day for a week. At the time, I wasn't very experienced in deliverance and was just doing my very best to follow the voice of the Holy Spirit to help her. At the end of the week, she was only seeing one huge snake. This snake was lying on her as she woke up. Later on, I understood that this snake was the head demon and the other snakes were its sidekicks. Because I wasn't very knowledgeable, experienced, or discerning, I didn't know the order to follow. That major principality finally left her because she didn't give up and was extremely desperate. Once and for all, she was free. She was free from medication. She was free from the mental institution. She was filled with joy and gratitude.

Through an event or a series of events, one demon usually opens the door to his friends. For example, a little boy is abandoned by his father. Abandonment opens the door to rejection, anger, bitterness, unforgiveness, self-hatred, insecurity, and more. In another example, a young girl is raped. This tragic event opens a door to shame and guilt, anger, fear, insecurity, unforgiveness, bitterness, self-hatred, and possibly hatred of others.

Below is a list of common groups of demons, along with the manifestations or symptoms that characterize them. When doing deliverance, once you recognize one of them, you may very likely need to cast out the others mentioned in the group also. One of them is usually the door opener to the team of demons.

Rebellion

- Pride
- Arrogance
- Accusations
- Slander
- Resistance
- Witchcraft
- Stubbornness
- Disobedience
- Self-will
- Resentment of authority
- Breaking ranks

Lies and Deception

- Manipulation
- Fear
- Control
- Fantasy
- Disillusionment
- Denial
- Defensiveness
- Twisted thinking
- Autism
- Learning disabilities
- Social awkwardness
- Deaf and dumb
- Leviathan

Unforgiveness

- Bitterness
- Resentment
- Hatred
- Anger
- Murder
- Temptation
- Slander
- Violence

Control

- Witchcraft
- Manipulation
- Dominance
- Possessiveness
- Jezebel

Insecurity

- Inferiority
- Pride
- Self-hatred
- Jealousy
- Timidity
- Self-pity
- Shyness
- Orphan spirit

Jealousy

- Envy
- Covetousness
- Comparison
- Extreme competitiveness
- Suspicion
- Selfishness
- Self-worship

Depression

- Despair
- Heaviness
- Loneliness
- Self-pity
- Death
- Hopelessness
- Suicide
- Insomnia
- Forgetfulness
- Passivity
- Withdrawal
- Fatigue
- Isolation

Passivity

- Funk
- Indifference
- Laziness
- Fatigue
- Victim mentality
- Pessimism
- Hopelessness
- Depression

Retaliation

- Rudeness
- Cruelty
- Anger
- Abuse
- Intimidation

- Sadism
- Hurt
- Sarcasm
- Bullying

Fear

- Worry
- Anxiety
- Dread
- Apprehension
- Terror

- Torment
- Trauma
- Rejection
- Seizures
- Paranoia

Competitiveness

- Ego
- Comparison
- Pride
- Vanity
- Anger

- Defensiveness
- Emotionalism
- Self-centeredness
- Insecurity
- Arrogance

Anger

- Frustration
- Impatience
- Intolerance

- Pressure
- Stress
- Disappointment

Addictive/Compulsive

- Alcoholism
- Drug abuse
- Gluttony
- Nicotine
- Nervousness
- Hurt

- Insecurity
- Inferiority
- Self-hatred
- Self-pity
- Drama (addiction to drama)

Fatigue

- Laziness
- Tiredness
- Weariness
- False burden

- False compassion
- Depression
- Heaviness

Accusation

- Slander
- Murder
- Anger
- Gossip

- Hatred
- Persecution
- Condemnation
- Strife

Guilt/Shame

- Condemnation
- Unworthiness
- Self-hatred

- Embarrassment
- Self-consciousness

False Burden/False Compassion

- People-pleaser
- Approval addiction
- Religious spirit
- Sadness
- Weariness

- Fatigue
- Depression
- Tiredness
- Heaviness
- Lies and deception

Grief

- Fear
- Sorrow
- Sadness
- Excessive crying

- Anger
- Loneliness
- Heaviness
- Depression

Pride

- Perfectionism
- Skepticism
- Arrogance
- Accusations
- Slander
- Resistance
- Resentment of authority

- Breaking ranks
- Defensiveness
- Super spiritualism/ spiritual pride
- Anger
- Impatience
- Self-centeredness
- Self-reward

Infirmity

- Sickness
- Depression

- Death
- Early deaths

Restlessness

- Extreme drive
- Workaholic
- Perfectionism
- Insecurity
- Nervousness

- Worry
- Anxiety
- Tormenting spirits
- False burdens

Covetousness

- Greed
- Selfishness
- Jealousy
- Envy
- Anger
- Gossip

- Slander
- Discontent
- Comparison
- Competition
- Insecurity
- Inferiority

Cults

- Jehovah's witnesses
- Christian Science
- Mormonism
- Unity
- Scientology
- Unitarians
- Wicca
- Meditation
- Kabbalah
- Luciferianism
- Satanism
- All eastern spiritual practices/ other cults

Occults

- Lies and deception
- Witchcraft
- All the occult practices mentioned before
- False idols
- Familiar spirits

False Religions

- Islam
- Roman Orthodox
- Jehovah's Witness
- Mormonism
- Buddhism
- Hinduism
- Other:
  » Lies and deception
  » Witchcraft
  » False idols

Cursing

- Blasphemy
- Mockery
- Sarcasm
- Anger
- Frustration
- Intolerance
- Agitation
- Nervousness

Lust

- Sexual immorality
- Masturbation
- Adultery
- Harlotry
- Whoredom
- Pornography
- Perversion
- Seduction
- Fantasy
- Homosexuality
- Lesbianism
- Bisexualism
- Promiscuity
- Other

Mental Sicknesses

- Schizophrenia
- Autism
- Suspicion
- Paranoia
- Phobia
- Bipolar
- Manic
- Manic-depressive

Obsession/Idol Worship

The following disorders are rooted in abandonment, rejection, rape, molestation, inferiority, and abuse and are open doors to obsession with perfectionism and control:

- (OCD) Obsessive Compulsive Disorder
- Anorexia
- Bulimia
- Overeating/food addiction
- Obesity
- Cutting yourself
- Suicidal thoughts
- Panic attacks
- Anxiety
- Self-hatred
- Bitterness
- Unforgiveness

Idol Worship/Self-Worship

These manifest in the three following groups:

1. Superiority Complex

- Intellectualism
- Vanity
- Workaholic (competitiveness)
- Perfectionism
- Sarcasm
- Dark humor
- Racism
- Anger
- Cruelty
- Mockery

2. Inferiority Complex

- Insecurities
- Self-pity
- Victim mentality
- Anger
- Loneliness
- Orphan spirit

3. Sexual demons (including Jezebel)

- Seductiveness
- Lust
- Porn addiction
- Homosexuality
- Adultery
- Fornication
- Masturbation
- Incest
- Sexual fantasies
- Perverse language; sexual or dirty talk

Prejudice

- Racism
- Sexism
- Class prejudice
- Social status prejudice
- Vanity
- Anger

- Hostility
- Superiority or supremacy
- Spirit of lust and perversion
- Intellectualism
- Pride

Before I teach you more on deliverance, I would like to stop here and show you a very simple but powerful deliverance method. It is not difficult, my friend. Jesus made it simple on the cross for you. Any voice you are hearing that tells you otherwise is not the voice of God but the voice of the devil who wants to make it difficult and complicated for you. He is a liar. You need to believe. You need to declare and receive your freedom. Do not have any fear. Trust Jesus and His mercy. He will not let you down. It is His will for you to be free. He died for your freedom.

1. Pray: Ask the Holy Spirit to reveal to you which demonic group is influencing you and your behaviors.
2. Identify: Recognize the group of demons who are trying to control and destroy your life. It can be more than one group.
3. Repent and renounce: *Expel* them one by one.

Declaration

Declare this out loud:

> *I am a child of the Living God through my Lord and Savior Jesus Christ. Jesus Christ is the King of kings and Lord of lords. He*

is my deliverer, shield, defense, protector, sanctifier, and healer. I am free from all bondages, strongholds, and the dominion of darkness through Jesus' sacrifice on the cross. I declare that Jesus Christ is my Lord and I belong to Him wholly. I am set free from all bondages and from all the forces of the devil by the blood of Jesus. I am a child of the light as Jesus Christ is the Light, and no darkness can dwell in me. I repent from opening any doors to the devil and I close all the doors of my soul to the demonic realm in the Name of Jesus Christ. I have authority in my life given by my Lord Jesus to exercise power over the devil and all unclean spirits. I am washed by the blood of the perfect Lamb. I am cleansed and sanctified. I declare that Jesus lives inside of me and I belong to Him. From this day on, the enemy of my soul cannot come near to me or dwell in me. I praise You and exalt Your Name, Lord Jesus, for rescuing me, saving me, and setting me free.

Now we're going to go over the major demonic principalities mentioned in the Bible. We'll look at the characteristics of the major principalities of darkness. These are:

- Antichrist
- Leviathan
- Python
- Jezebel
- Ahab
- Judas

Spirit of Antichrist

Who is a liar but he who denies that Jesus is the Christ [Messiah]? *He is* **antichrist** *who denies the Father and the Son* (1 John 2:22 NKJV).

Who Is Antichrist?

Anti means against and in opposition and resistance to someone or something. Antichrist is a person and a demonic principality. As indicated by its name, it is anti; it opposes and deceives by imitating—in other words, a counterfeit of Christ the Messiah. This is a very deceiving spirit that operates even in churches and ministries (see 1 John 2:18).

Characteristics of Antichrist

1. Operates through lies and deception

For many deceivers have gone out into the world who do not confess Jesus Christ as coming in the flesh (2 John 1:7 NKJV).

This is a deceiver and an *antichrist*.

- Humanism—feminism and New Age
- Fake peace
- "Everyone worships the same god" doctrine
- Everyone will go to heaven
- There is no hell
- Jesus didn't die on the cross (Islamic teaching from the Koran) (see 1 John 2:22)

- Bible is altered and not trustworthy
- Jesus is the brother of Lucifer (Mormonism)
- Jesus was a good teacher (Jehovah's Witnesses)
- Jesus was one of the good gods (New Age Hinduism)
- All religions are the paths to truth
- Judaism's rejection of Jesus as Messiah
- Islam is a religion of peace
- Masons and other clubs or allegiances
- Occult practices

2. Persecutes the church and Christians

They will put you out of the synagogue; in fact, the time is coming when anyone who kills you will think they are offering a service to God (John 16:2).

As we can see in the media, through the violence of Islamic terrorist groups such as ISIS, Christians and churches are being persecuted by the Antichrist spirit. There is a fierce attack taking place against Christians.

3. Imitation and counterfeit

Satan himself masquerades as an angel of light (2 Corinthians 11:14).

Something or someone may look like they are from the throne of God but very well may be from the pits of hell. We need godly wisdom and discernment to distinguish between good and evil.

Remember in the Book of Exodus that up to a certain point Pharaoh's magicians were able to do the same miracles Moses was performing. Pharaoh represents the Antichrist in the Exodus story. He doesn't allow the children of God to worship their God. Antichrist wants to be worshiped. It is the very spirit of Satan. As in the wilderness, the last temptation of Jesus was Satan offering Him all the kingdoms of the world in return for worshiping him.

Imitation always comes after the original. Including the devil, no one can create from nothing as God does. When we create something, we create it based on tools that were created. In the same way, the devil takes something that God created, then twists, imitates, and counterfeits it. This is why we, as believers, must be very careful and seek the gift of discernment to know what is from God and what is from the devil.

Today, you can see in our land that evil is called good and accepted as such. The Word of God is very clear on this matter.

> **Woe to those** who call evil good and good evil, who put darkness for light and light for darkness, who put bitter for sweet and sweet for bitter (Isaiah 5:20).

The word *woe* is a curse. Whoever calls evil good and good evil brings a curse upon themselves. No matter how good and alluring something may be, we need to seek the Holy Spirit's guidance for wisdom and discernment.

> As the heavens are higher than the earth, so are my ways higher than your ways and my thoughts than your thoughts (Isaiah 55:9).

We cannot rely on our own understanding. We need to seek the Holy Spirit, the Spirit of Truth, to reveal God's truth.

> Trust in the Lord with all your heart and lean not on your own understanding (Proverbs 3:5).

Something appearing to be good, acceptable, or beautiful doesn't necessarily mean it is from God. Many believers are deceived by the devil and live in corrupted and perverse lifestyles, justifying their ways with their own wisdom, which is worldly and demonic. They are heading to destruction and refuse to listen to godly counsel. They will defend their way of living with all their might, and if you try to warn them they will accuse you of being intolerant and not loving or graceful. However, God doesn't change His truth according to our likings and opinions. It is foolish to try to change God and make Him what we want Him to be. Unless people submit to Him and seek His ways and obey His commands, they are heading into a very dangerous place, if not there already.

> *There is a way that appears to be right, but in the end **it leads to death*** (Proverbs 14:12).

This is a very crafty familiar spirit that operates under a "good cause" mask to deceive many. It speaks kind, loving, and caring words and seeks peace, but it is a vicious spirit to destroy many. This spirit:

- Offers lust instead of love
- Allows perversion and murders (abortions) under the mask of freedom
- Divides nations under the mask of peace
- Is pleasing to the eye as the forbidden fruit in the garden—it is very tactful, intellectual, smart, diplomatic, politically correct, and seductive

4. *Accusing and slanderous (see Revelation 13:5)*

The devil is called the accuser of the brethren and accuses God's children day and night (see Rev. 12:10). His other name is *slanderer*. Strong's

Greek Concordance #1228 states the word used for him is *diabolos*, meaning slanderous, the slanderer, and false accuser.

> *Lord, who may dwell in your sacred tent? Who may live on your holy mountain? The one whose walk is blameless, who does what is righteous, who speaks the truth from their heart; whose tongue utters no slander, who does no wrong to a neighbor, and casts no slur on others* (Psalm 15:1-3).

> *Whoever **slanders** their neighbor in secret, I will put to silence; whoever has haughty eyes and a proud heart, I will not tolerate* (Psalm 101:5).

> *May **slanderers** not be established in the land; may disaster hunt down the violent* (Psalm 140:11).

No matter how many wrongs people may have done to you, or despite the falsehood you may see in them, be very, very careful not to operate in this spirit—the demon of accusation and slander—because that is the very characteristic of the devil.

I used to be very accusing toward my husband, and later on the Holy Spirit convicted me through the warning of a close friend who held me accountable and was also a wise and godly counselor. She told me that my accusing tongue against my husband was bringing a curse into our marriage, health, and finances. I immediately repented and renounced all my accusations. From that moment on, my marriage blossomed and we started prospering in every area of our lives. In the same way, I stopped accusing other people or preachers, and I have seen showers of blessings being poured out by God into our lives. The spirit of accusation is a big demonic force in the church today. As followers of Christ, we need to refrain from opening a door to this demonic force.

Some people justify their accusations as exposing evil, which we are commanded to do in the Bible. I used to justify my accusations that way too, until one day the Holy Spirit said to me, "Why don't you start exposing the evil first within yourself? You still have areas that are not in submission to My voice. Then you can obey this command with mercy and love toward others." That was a huge eye-opener for me.

5. *Craves for power and position (see Revelation 13:3)*

Lucifer was kicked out from heaven because he wanted to sit on the throne of God.

> *I will ascend above the tops of the clouds; I will make myself like the Most High* (Isaiah 14:14).

In Genesis 3, the serpent told Eve if she ate the fruit, she was going to be like God. We must be very vigilant about the root of our desire for power and position. The highest position in the Kingdom of God is being a servant. God's biggest compliment to His obedient children is to call them "My servant." Going up in the Kingdom of God starts by going down. Desire to gain high position, fame, and power is the root of selfish ambition and opens a door to the demonic.

We must follow the example of Jesus Christ as Paul stated in his letter to the Philippian church:

> *Therefore if you have any encouragement from being united with Christ, if any comfort from his love, if any common sharing in the Spirit, if any tenderness and compassion, then make my joy complete by being like-minded, having the same love, being one in spirit and of one mind. Do nothing out of selfish ambition or vain conceit. Rather, in humility value others above yourselves,*

not looking to your own interests but each of you to the interests of the others.

In your relationships with one another, have the same mindset as Christ Jesus:

Who, being in very nature God, did not consider equality with God something to be used to his own advantage; rather, he made himself nothing by taking the very nature of a servant, being made in human likeness. And being found in appearance as a man, he humbled himself by becoming obedient to death— even death on a cross!

Therefore God exalted him to the highest place and gave him the name that is above every name, that at the name of Jesus every knee should bow, in heaven and on earth and under the earth, and every tongue acknowledge that Jesus Christ is Lord, to the glory of God the Father (Philippians 2:1-11).

6. Bloodthirsty and murderous

*Be alert and of sober mind. Your enemy the devil prowls around like a roaring lion **looking for someone to devour*** (1 Peter 5:8).

Also, John 10:10 states that the thief comes to kill, steal, and destroy. His major purpose is to kill. He is after your life. He doesn't only oppress you and depress you, but eventually wants to bring you to a place of suicide. This is the very reason you need to slay the devil at the very beginning of feeling oppressed or depressed.

In the Bible, Daniel's life was in danger because he didn't bow down to the king's statue. Jezebel, who operated under the rank of this principality, tried to kill Elijah. Pharisees and Jewish religious leaders who were after killing Jesus operated under this spirit.

Today we see in our nation millions of unborn babies being murdered through abortion. The spirit of Antichrist is behind these mass murders. Also around the world today, countless Christians are being martyred through the actions of this principality.

7. Crafty and smart

The serpent was the craftiest of all the animals who were in the garden in Genesis 3. Ever since the garden, the devil is still trying to accomplish his plan of destruction for those who follow his ways.

Today, one of the ways we see this deception taking place, even in the church, is through intellectualism. The Antichrist spirit is very intellectual, diplomatic, and tactful, and may appear very sophisticated and eloquent.

8. Mocking and insulting

Mockery and insults toward the children and servants of God are other evidences of the Antichrist spirit. Another evidence that the Antichrist spirit is at work is mockery of the message of the Gospel and of preachers who spread the good news. The Bible talks about mockers in various places.

> Blessed is the one who does not walk in step with the wicked or stand in the way that sinners take or sit in the company of mockers (Psalm 1:1).

> But when Sanballat the Horonite, Tobiah the Ammonite official and Geshem the Arab heard about it, they **mocked** and ridiculed us. "What is this you are doing?" they asked. "Are you rebelling against the king?" (Nehemiah 2:19)

Nehemiah was rebuilding the walls of Jerusalem. He was serving the God of Israel with great zeal and reverence when the enemy started coming against him with mockery.

*Then twisted together a crown of thorns and set it on his head. They put a staff in his right hand. Then they knelt in front of him and **mocked** him. "Hail, king of the Jews!" they said* (Matthew 27:29).

*After they had **mocked** him, they took off the robe and put his own clothes on him. Then they led him away to crucify him* (Matthew 27:31).

*In the same way the chief priests, the teachers of the law and the elders **mocked** him* (Matthew 27:41).

9. Seductive

Starting in the garden, the serpent presents sin in a beautifully wrapped package. It is the Antichrist's old tactic to present something deadly on a beautiful golden plate that's hard to resist.

Satan himself masquerades as an angel of light (2 Corinthians 11:14).

He always offers something extraordinarily and exceptionally beautiful in return for your soul. He knows your weaknesses and trigger points. He knows which bait to use for which fish to catch for his wicked scheme.

10. Lawless

He doesn't have any rules or standards (see Dan. 7:25). He will go to any and every level or path to kill, steal, and destroy.

We also know that the law is made not for the righteous but for lawbreakers and rebels, the ungodly and sinful, the unholy and irreligious, for those who kill their fathers or mothers, for murderers (1 Timothy 1:9).

11. Prideful and boastful

*How you have fallen from heaven, morning star, son of the dawn! You have been cast down to the earth, you who once laid low the nations! You said in your heart, **"I will ascend to the heavens; I will raise my throne above the stars of God; I will sit enthroned on the mount of assembly, on the utmost heights of Mount Zaphon. I will ascend above the tops of the clouds; I will make myself like the Most High"** (Isaiah 14:12-14).*

If you notice, "I" (*ego*) is the center of Lucifer's speech. It is boastful talk. As Christians, we need to be very careful that our faith declarations line up with God's Word instead of the "name it and claim it" Lucifer boastfulness, which is an offense to God Almighty (see 2 Thess. 2:3-4). Everything we declare and decree has to be in submission to God's will and must be done in humility and with a pure heart.

Let no one deceive you in any way; for that day will not come unless the rebellion comes first and the lawless one is revealed, the one destined for destruction.... The coming of the lawless one is apparent in the working of Satan, who uses all power, signs, lying wonders, and every kind of wicked deception for those who are perishing, because they refused to love the truth and so be saved (2 Thessalonians 2:3, 9-10 NRSV).

*Every spirit that does not confess that Jesus Christ has come in the flesh is not of God. And this is the spirit of the **Antichrist**, which you have heard was coming, and is now already in the world* (1 John 4:3 NKJV).

12. Lying and deception

Jesus said when the devil speaks his native language, he is lying. Lying, deception, twisting words, manipulation, pretention, falsehood, cheating, and exaggeration (overstatement, dramatization, and overemphasis) are rooted in the devil's DNA.

> *You are the offspring of your father, the devil, and you serve your father very well, passionately carrying out his desires. He's been a murderer right from the start! He never stood with the One who is the true Prince, for he's full of nothing but lies—lying is his native tongue. He is a master of deception and the father of lies!* (John 8:44 TPT)

Highest in the demonic hierarchy of Satan's kingdom is the Antichrist spirit. Today we see this principality operating in Muslim as well as communist nations. Humanism has its origin in the spirit of Antichrist also, which offers a counterfeit peace for all.

Demonic peace appears in the form of "all religions worship the same god" beliefs, in militant feminism, and more, and all come from the spirit of Antichrist. This is a very intellectual personality that worships education, titles, and power, and usually has sarcasm and mockery in it. Atheism is also a huge division of Antichrist.

This spirit also uses constant accusations but operates in very intellectual and elite circles. It hates any form of godliness and holiness.

The Antichrist spirit approves of worldliness and carnality in any shape and form and delights in carnal joking and insults. This spirit mocks, perverts, and twists the truth.

Even in churches and religious organizations, false believers (wolves in sheep's clothing) operate with the spirit of Antichrist. The Pharisee spirit also comes from the Antichrist spirit, which is a counterfeit. Remember, the Pharisees were against Christ, which is translated Antichrist.

> *Beloved, do not believe every spirit, but test the spirits to see whether they are from God; for many false prophets have gone out into the world. By this you know the Spirit of God: every spirit that confesses that Jesus Christ has come in the flesh is from God, and every spirit that does not confess Jesus is not from God. And this is the spirit of the antichrist, of which you have heard that it is coming; and now it is already in the world. Little children, you are from God, and have conquered them; for the one who is in you is greater than the one who is in the world. They are from the world; therefore what they say is from the world, and the world listens to them. We are from God. Whoever knows God listens to us, and whoever is not from God does not listen to us. From this we know the spirit of truth and the spirit of error* (1 John 4:1-6 NRSV).

How to deal with this principality?

Remember, no matter how strong or powerful the principality of darkness is, our God is bigger and stronger and has given us authority through Jesus Christ to overcome them. Pay attention that the name of the spirit is *Antichrist*; therefore everything that is centered in Jesus Christ will crush him. So lift up the name of Jesus at every opportunity.

- Bind the spirit of Antichrist, then release the Holy Spirit's truth and power into the situation (see Matt. 16:19).
- Apply the blood of Christ (see Rev. 12:11).

- Declare your position and your place as a child of the living God (see Rev. 12:11).

- Live in complete obedience to the Word of God. The devil lost his position in heaven due to his pride, which led to rebellion. Humility and obedience to God will defeat the devil immediately. You need to show him who your boss is and you need to mean it, demonstrating it through your behavior.

- Command that spirit to flee from you!

   Submit yourselves, then, to God. Resist the devil, and he will flee from you (James 4:7).

The Spirit of Python: The Demonic Serpent

The Python spirit is a demonic principality (high-ranking demonic force) connected to the spirit of divination (false, counterfeit prophecy), which always attacks the true prophetic voice ordained and sourced by God (see Acts 16:16-18). A shortcut antidote is to declare God's Word and praise and worship *out loud*. Divination and witchcraft open the doors to this principality of darkness and it grows as it's fed by divination through false prophecies. Also, controlling personalities who force their way in and then operate in prophecies and words of knowledge in the demonic realm fall under the spirit of Python. This principality has an assignment—to choke your voice and God's vision in your life, then to paralyze and ultimately kill you.

People who are blended so well with Python or operating under its power come into your life as if they're a blessing and support to you. Then they find your weaknesses by presenting themselves as friends who want the best for you and want to help you succeed in your God-given mission. After they learn your weaknesses, they try to destroy you. This is one of the major vicious demonic principalities. The Python demon finds its entry through false religions, occult practices, New Age, witchcraft, sorcery, divination, medium readings, and other deceiving religious practices.

In Judges 16, Delilah played the major role in Samson's death, operating through the Python spirit. Samson had a divine calling and destination. The devil wanted to take him out before Samson fulfilled God's destiny for him.

> *So Delilah said to Samson, "Tell me the secret of your great strength and how you can be tied up and subdued"* (Judges 16:6).

Just like its name, *Python,* this spirit is an extremely crafty and sneaky demonic power that enters in through a person's blind side. This demon tries to remain unnoticed as much as possible, and therefore it is hard to identify and expel. They first hatch through thoughts and speak to people's minds. Your mind has ears. This spirit whispers evil thoughts over time. It is a patient, demonic force that takes its course slowly. It brings to your mind all kinds of negativity and despair, then releases increasing doses of evil and injects its poison into your system. People don't commit crimes overnight. They don't commit suicide after just thinking of it that day. They don't decide to cheat on their spouses as soon as they meet an attractive individual. The Python spirit has hatched its eggs in the mind a long time ago, then strikes when the time and the opportunity present themselves.

> *Then, after desire has conceived, it gives birth to sin; and sin, when it is full-grown, gives birth to death* (James 1:15).

Divination is the foundation of the spirit of Python. Someone who is constantly prophesying and operating under the power of divination instead of the Holy Spirit is very likely possessed by this spirit. We see that this spirit is named in Acts 16:

> And it came to pass in our going on to prayer, a certain maid, having a spirit of Python, did meet us, who brought much employment to her masters by soothsaying, she having followed Paul and us, was crying, saying, "These men are servants of the Most High God, who declare to us a way of salvation;" and this she was doing for many days, but Paul having been grieved, and having turned, said to the spirit, "I command thee, in the name of Jesus Christ, to come forth from her;" and it came forth the same hour (Acts 16:16-18 YLT).

If you notice, this girl was telling the truth: "These men are the servants of the Most High God." This spirit takes the truth and fashions it with evil and even flatters. True servants of God don't seek or need the flattery or validation of others. They're secure in their calling and identity, just as Paul didn't give in to the fortune-teller's praise.

The devil knows the truth and hates it. Remember he used the Word of God to tempt Jesus in the wilderness (see Matt. 4).

There are many people in the *church* today who operate by twisting and manipulating the Word of God for their advantage, like this girl. They possess great knowledge of the Word of God, they can quote Scriptures right and left, and they still carry the spirit of Python within them. The religious and legalistic spirits are evidences of the presence of this spirit. Their works and supernatural moves are counterfeit. They know how to imitate godliness and religion.

As you notice from the Scripture, the girl was a fortune teller. The spirit of Python operates with witchcraft— "counterfeit and familiar spirits." This spirit imitates God's work to a certain extent. Remember in the Book of Exodus that to a certain degree, Pharaoh's magicians could do the same miraculous signs Moses and Aaron were performing. This spirit can operate in the physical realm as well as the spiritual. This is the very reason we all need discernment and must test the spirits.

> *Dear friends, do not believe every spirit, but test the spirits to see whether they are from God, because many false prophets have gone out into the world. This is how you can recognize the Spirit of God: Every spirit that acknowledges that Jesus Christ has come in the flesh is from God, but every spirit that does not acknowledge Jesus is not from God. This is the spirit of the antichrist, which you have heard is coming and even now is already in the world* (1 John 4:1-3).

Evidence of a Python Spirit

- Breathing problems (Python suffocates)
- Paralysis
- Pacification
- Stolen joy and strength
- Mind battles: Python hatches hundreds of eggs—seeds of defeat, hatred, lust, bitterness, sadness, negativity, and fear
- Fatigue—extreme busyness leads to exhaustion
- Dizziness
- Forgetfulness
- Scattered-mindedness or air-headedness

- Lack of desire to open your mouth to pray
- Clutter in the mind
- Cloudy mind, cannot think clearly
- Python steals the wind and move of the Holy Spirit through prophecy
- Heaviness on the chest
- Loss of voice
- Vision problems—Python attacks your physical and spiritual vision
- Oppression
- Depression
- Suicidal thoughts
- Flattery—Python brings you to pride, just as the girl following Paul was flattering him with the truth but validating him through a demonic spirit
- False prophecy
- Not wanting to be corrected—prideful people
- Desire to use you to destroy you (Python has a demonic assignment)
- Extreme sorrow and sadness bringing passivity
- Imitation of your gifting and your gifts
- Manipulation
- Strife
- Hate peace and unity

You Must Praise and Worship Out Loud to Destroy Python

Paul and Silas prayed and sang hymns, and their chains were broken.

But at midnight Paul and Silas were praying and singing hymns to God, and the prisoners were listening to them. Suddenly there was a great earthquake, so that the foundations of the prison were shaken; and immediately all the doors were opened and everyone's chains were loosed. And the keeper of the prison, awaking from sleep and seeing the prison doors open, supposing the prisoners had fled, drew his sword and was about to kill himself. But Paul called with a loud voice, saying, "Do yourself no harm, for we are all here" (Acts 16:25-28 NKJV).

The major cure to kick out the spirit of Python is praise and worship. The spirit of Python cannot stand confession, praise, worship, and reading the Word out loud.

As strong as this demonic principality is, it can be bound in Jesus' Name as if it were nothing. It operates by fear. Do not fear this spirit if you are doing deliverance on yourself or on another person. Take your authority in Jesus Christ. First declare and decree, then proclaim the Word of God.

One *very important point* I would like to bring to your attention: "Every spirit that acknowledges that Jesus Christ has come in the flesh is from God" (1 John 4:2). When we declare this word, there is more to it than lip service, because even demons acknowledge who Jesus Christ is, as we see in the New Testament during Jesus' encounter with demons.

I have seen demonized people who acknowledged this, which made me search and pray for more revelation on this Scripture. Then God revealed to me that the word *acknowledge* is more than recognition or even accepting. The word *acknowledge* is submitting, yielding, worshiping, and exalting. Demons don't do that. They are in rebellion. Sometimes God's people fall into misunderstanding and tell the demonized person to confess that Jesus Christ is Lord. Yes, it works in many cases, but not all. That is not evidence enough to determine whether someone is set free. Demons are very tricky.

In my personal experience, the greatest evidence that a person is free from demons is vocalized worship. Many people start worshiping God out loud as soon as they are set free.

With the spirit of Python comes the spirit of seduction. There was a girl I knew from childhood who had a spirit of Python. She wrecked the marriage of very dear friends in our circle; she was giving a secret dose of seduction to the married men around us, and even those men weren't aware of it. Wherever I took her, she would get close with a married man. I didn't understand at the beginning, because this girl looked and acted like an angel. She looked like the purest thing, but was secretly into a porn fantasy world and adultery. When God exposed her, to my shock she confessed everything, then ran away. Afterward, her seductive communications with other married men were found. Python is a very sneaky and alluring personality.

This spirit is also very manipulative and comes with the victim mentality. People who carry this spirit have a lot of fear and anxiety, as well as panic attacks, various speech impediments, breathing problems, irregular heartbeats, fatigue, sleeping disorders, depression, suicidal thoughts, and suicide attempts.

Whenever you speak or interact with someone who has the spirit of Python, you feel extreme heaviness and/or tiredness and even exhaustion afterward. Personalities with this spirit have a suffocating effect. If you are living with someone with this spirit, then odds are very high that you may struggle with depression and suicidal thoughts. The spirit of death enters in through this.

The spirit of Python attacks or attaches itself to people who are prophetic and who have a preaching and teaching anointing. This spirit tries everything to stop you from speaking up. It is after your voice. Therefore, it is crucial for you to praise and worship God out loud.

Python is an oppressive spirit. Demonic oppression and depression are the results of this spirit, as is suicide. The Muslim world is operating through the oppression of Python, which originates from Antichrist.

Because this spirit operates through mind and emotion control, many emotional and mental abusers fall into this category. People who operate under the spirit of Python are very demanding, overpowering, and intimidating people. Oftentimes, however, strong leaders have been wrongly accused of this, which is why we have to use discernment. Let's face it—we live in a hurting world with a lot of wounded individuals, and when a healthy, strong, and free leader comes to the scene, he or she will intimidate and offend a lot of people because of the authority he or she is exercising.

However, there are also victims of the Python spirit who love to go under the wings of strong, godly leaders such as David or Deborah. Not every strong leader has this spirit, so the enemy likes to sneak into the leadership through weaker, demonically oppressed or possessed personalities to destroy great leaders. David's right-hand man, Joab, had a Python spirit. The biggest target is always those in leadership. Always.

Spirit of Jezebel

Nevertheless I have a few things against you, because you allow that woman Jezebel, who calls herself a prophetess, to teach and seduce My servants to commit sexual immorality and eat things sacrificed to idols (Revelation 2:20 NKJV).

First we need to understand the characteristics of Jezebel herself. Jezebel was an extremely vicious but super-spiritual personality in the Bible. The books of First and Second Kings talk about Jezebel. She hated Elijah and wanted to kill him. She threw threats at him. Now remember, Elijah had prayed, fire from heaven had come down, and hundreds of false prophets were put to the sword, yet he was running away from this woman. The Jezebel spirit is a murderous spirit. It wants to kill, literally, or murder someone's reputation through gossip and slander.

Jezebel was the daughter of Ethbaal, king of the Sidonians, who worshiped Baal. She was given in marriage to Ahab, just like a piece of property (see 1 Kings 16:31). This is the background of Jezebel. She was rejected and abandoned by her father as though she were nothing, and given in marriage to a man in another land.

When Naboth refused to sell his vineyard to King Ahab, she wrote a letter forging her husband's signature, called them to a fast (a spiritual, religious activity), and she brought false witnesses against Naboth to cause him to be put to death based on Jewish law. So this spirit would do anything to murder you, your soul, your body, or your reputation if she doesn't get her way (see 1 Kings 21).

Women or men with deep past hurts and wounds have open doors to the spirit of Jezebel. Usually these people have survived by their own ways and means to make it in life and have become very self-dependent, strong, controlling, intimidating, demanding, and rough. They lie and manipulate to get their way and to look good. They have serious, deeply rooted anger inside them.

People with the Jezebel spirit are extremely needy and insecure, and they don't like or respect boundaries! They hate when someone tells them "no" or sets boundaries. They control through manipulation, pity, and guilt. They play the victim to manipulate and want to be in charge or at the center of your life, often demanding more of your time and attention. If they can't control you, it will drive them crazy.

People with the Jezebel spirit usually get close to the leadership and look for people in authority and power to find some sort of security because they're very insecure and rejected people. Through the Jezebel spirit, the devil aims to hurt leaders. These are very spiritual, even prophetic people (through familiar spirits). The enemy loves to distract people from their true calling. He often uses very hurt people to devastate ministries and ignorant leaders. Jezebel often has an obsession with one or more individuals at a time. She craves for attention.

If you are around a person with a Jezebel spirit, you will get extreme tiredness, fatigue, anxiety, lack of joy, and even depression can sneak in suddenly. They will suffocate you without you noticing, and you will wonder why.

If you are going to do deliverance of a person with a Jezebel spirit, be very careful, because they usually say they need deliverance but don't want it. They will even lie to look good to you instead of telling the truth to get delivered. Most of the time all they want is attention. The major demonic powers over them are lies, deception, and manipulation. They're in disillusionment and denial. Pride plays a major role in their denial. Just make sure they truly want deliverance; otherwise the devil will just use them to distract you, steal your time, and hurt you. If you don't seek the Holy Spirit's discernment, you can even get sick. I'm not trying to scare you but to prepare you. As in the example of Elijah, Jezebel is after the life of a spiritual leader. The goal of this spirit is to bring depression and suicidal thoughts to the mind of the person they're influencing, just as it happened to Elijah.

Remember, every Jezebel needs an Ahab. Ahab is the passive, wicked personality. Usually people with the Jezebel spirit find a very wounded person to control under the mask of helping them.

The spirit of Jezebel brings sickness, and most of the time doctors cannot diagnose the problem. If you are the one who has the spirit of Jezebel, repent and be delivered from it following the guidelines I am offering you in this book. Confession and repentance are the keys.

If you are dealing with a Jezebel personality, because they are driven by power and control, *set strong boundaries* to protect yourself, even though they will hate your boundaries. You cannot tolerate Jezebel in your life. Refuse to live in fear of this spirit, and stop bowing down to it. You also need to repent from obeying an individual who has this spirit instead of obeying and submitting to God. If you are submitting to Jezebel, you are most likely a people-pleaser with deep roots in the pain of rejection. You need to be first delivered and healed from the soul wounds, then repent and be free from obeying Jezebel. Cover yourself at every opportunity with the blood of Christ Jesus through prayer. Read the Word out loud, praise, and worship.

Characteristics of Jezebel

1. Controlling and pushy personality (telling King Ahab what to do)

> *Then Jezebel his wife said to him, "You now exercise authority over Israel! Arise, eat food, and let your heart be cheerful; I will give you the vineyard of Naboth the Jezreelite"* (1 Kings 21:7 NKJV).

2. Manipulative and lying

And she wrote letters in Ahab's name, sealed them with his seal, and sent the letters to the elders and the nobles who were dwelling in the city with Naboth. She wrote in the letters, saying, Proclaim a fast, and seat Naboth with high honor among the people; and seat two men, scoundrels, before him to bear witness against him, saying, "You have blasphemed God and the king." Then take him out, and stone him, that he may die (1 Kings 21:8-10 NKJV).

3. Attention seeker

Now when Jehu had come to Jezreel, Jezebel heard of it; and she put paint on her eyes and adorned her head, and looked through a window (2 Kings 9:30 NKJV).

4. Murderous spirit (slanders and gossips)

Then take him out, and stone him, that he may die (1 Kings 21:10 NKJV).

*Was it not reported to my lord what I did when **Jezebel** killed the prophets of the Lord, how I hid one hundred men of the Lord's prophets, fifty to a cave, and fed them with bread and water?* (1 Kings 18:13 NKJV)

5. Intimidating and bullying personality (threatened the prophet Elijah)

*Then **Jezebel** sent a messenger to Elijah, saying, "So let the gods do to me, and more also, if I do not make your life as the life* *of one of them by tomorrow about this time"* (1 Kings 19:2 NKJV).

6. Super spiritual

Jezebel is a self-proclaimed prophetess. But she is a a false prophet who operates through familiar, unclean spirits to prophesy.

> *And it came to pass, as though it had been a trivial thing for him to walk in the sins of Jeroboam the son of Nebat, that he took as wife **Jezebel** the daughter of Ethbaal, king of the Sidonians; and he went and served Baal and worshiped him* (1 Kings 16:31 NKJV).

> *Now therefore, send and gather all Israel to me on Mount Carmel, the four hundred and fifty prophets of Baal, and the four hundred prophets of Asherah, who eat at **Jezebel's** table* (1 Kings 18:19 NKJV).

7. Seductive

> *But there was no one like Ahab who sold himself to do wickedness in the sight of the Lord, because **Jezebel** his wife stirred him up* (1 Kings 21:25 NKJV).

> *Nevertheless I have a few things against you, because you allow that woman **Jezebel**, who calls herself a prophetess, to teach and seduce My servants to commit sexual immorality and eat things sacrificed to idols. And I gave her time to repent of her sexual immorality, and she did not repent. Indeed I will cast her into a sickbed, and those who commit adultery with her into great tribulation, unless they repent of their deeds. I will kill her children with death, and all the churches shall know that I am*

He who searches the minds and hearts. And I will give to each one of you according to your works (Revelation 2:20-23 NKJV).

8. Temperamental and emotionally unstable

The Jezebel spirit shows extreme emotions and temperament, gets easily offended, and can't take correction because of pride.

9. Witchcraft (cursed the prophet Elijah)

The Jezebel spirit puts curses on people, ministries, and anything that is in her way. She seeks revenge and calls it a vindication.

> *Now it happened, when Joram saw Jehu, that he said, "Is it peace, Jehu?" So he answered, "What peace, as long as the harlotries of your mother **Jezebel** and her witchcraft are so many?"* (2 Kings 9:22 NKJV)

10. Rebellious

Jezebel hates to be under authority. If she is not the authority, she finds every excuse to not submit and rebels against authority. As in the Bible, Jezebel imitated and usurped Ahab's authority, this demon imitates authority without the title and breaks the ranks.

11. Power seeker—always close to the leadership

Jezebel wants power in order to feel important. This demon operates close to the leadership. In the Bible, she was married to King Ahab.

12. Persecutes the church, godly leaders, and prophets

> *For so it was, while **Jezebel** massacred the prophets of the Lord, that Obadiah had taken one hundred prophets and hidden*

them, fifty to a cave, and had fed them with bread and water
(1 Kings 18:4 NKJV).

13. *Doesn't respect boundaries—*
   can't take no for an answer

If you are dealing with this demon in a person, you can identify Jezebel by setting boundaries. Jezebel doesn't respect or like boundaries set by other people. She is pushy and uses emotionalism to manipulate.

Spirit of Ahab

This is a passive, wicked spirit. This personality doesn't hear or seek truth and only likes what is convenient. Many Ahabs, in my experience, have a deaf and dumb spirit. They appear very graceful, but on the contrary they have a vicious and sarcastic dark side. If there is an Ahab, there is always a Jezebel. Secretaries, pastors' wives, or pastors and very high-ranking people in the ministry or Christian organizations often have this spirit. They like Jezebel's charm and will support what is wicked and deny what is righteous. Money, power, and stature are what they worship. They love their comfort zones, and anything that's inconvenient to them is their enemy.

Many wives of Ahabs are in deep depression and often suicidal. Ahabs don't take responsibility to take action. They are usually faultfinders and stingy in encouragement. They put work before family, and their friendships are based on mutual gain. Ahabs do good deeds to feel good about themselves because they are task- and score-driven, but their actions are robotic and not in tune with the Holy Spirit.

Spirit of Leviathan: Monstrous Sea Serpent

In that day the Lord with His severe sword, great and strong, will punish Leviathan the fleeing serpent, Leviathan that twisted serpent; and He will slay the reptile that is in the sea (Isaiah 27:1 NKJV).

He beholds every high thing; **he** [Leviathan] **is king over all the children of pride** (Job 41:34 NKJV).

This demonic principality operates through pride, is fed by pride, and mostly obtains access to an individual through ancestral pride as an inherited generational attachment. Leviathan *has* a thief personality because he constantly steals, and the first thing he tries to steal is the power and glory of God.

People who are under the control of Leviathan seek personal glory versus God's glory and power. After God's glory, Leviathan mostly goes after stealing your resources, gifts, talents, time, money, destiny, potential, inheritance, and all your blessings. Leviathan influences you to make foolish decisions, based on your ego and pride, to waste your finances. Leviathan causes people to lose money instead of saving. Because the person is manipulated by his or her pride, their decisions are unwise and cost them big opportunities in life.

Unlike Python, Leviathan is a beating spirit. Python chokes; Leviathan beats you with its tail and wounds you with words. If you are always losing money, valuable things, opportunities, jobs, favor, and more, you need to dig deeper with the Lord to get to the bottom of it. If you feel like your purse has holes in it and you cannot save up money, even though you try harder and harder, you may be dealing with a Leviathan spirit. Leviathan chokes all of your finances, blessings, and opportunities. This spirit will generate a lot of frustration and anger in your life to cause you to give up, to have an anger outburst or extreme emotionalism, or to fail in your career or lose your job. This spirit can also bring depression and suicidal thoughts. If you are feeling stuck and are not fulfilling your dreams, calling, and potential, then it may be that you are dealing with a Leviathan spirit. It causes excessive spending, greed, and unnecessary financial loss.

Many individuals who have an open door to this spirit lack financial wisdom.

Characteristics of Leviathan

- Pride: Leviathan operates through pride, especially spiritual pride and arrogance
- Egotistical, boastful, and arrogant
- Deception: Leviathan twists words and intentions, is malicious and manipulative
- Vanity, importance of looks
- Self-seeking, self-pity, and self-advertising spirit (self-attachment, including self-pity, is idol worship)
- Poverty, lack, debt, famine, and barrenness
- Losing things, from small to big
- Prone to accidents and sickness
- Bankruptcy (in many cases)
- Inheritance loss or disputes for generations
- Leviathan operates through fear and threats
- Revengeful: Leviathan calls it vindication, because it twists words

- Thief, spirit of robbery: steals tithes, offerings, time, potential, destiny, and God's glory. This demonic principality tries to steal God's glory by seeking his personal glory.
- Boastful tongue and proud of being strong
- Entitlement, demands promotion
- Refuses correction and gets offended easily due to pride
- Plays blame games and lives with excuses because of pride
- Dominant, superior to everyone, knows it all
- Rude
- Faultfinder
- Defensive, hides sins, doesn't confess and is not humble
- Self-righteous accusations and blame games
- Judgmental, criticizing, and argumentative
- Seeks title and rank, not servanthood
- Has to be right all the time
- Rebellious, cannot surrender or submit, disrespects authority
- No accountability
- Slanderous and loves gossip
- Loves information to find weaknesses of people to manipulate and slander
- Drama queen—steals time with drama

People with the Leviathan spirit spend their money on unnecessary things rather than their needs and also have serious insecurity issues. Those who have obsessions with wearing expensive brand clothing; go to expensive movie theaters, concerts, and entertainment; and who cannot save money are very insecure people who have not been restored to their identity in Christ. They have open doors to Leviathan.

Can you draw out Leviathan with a hook,
Or snare his tongue with a line which you lower?
[Strong and prideful in his strength]
Can you put a reed through his nose,
[Disobedient]
Or pierce his jaw with a hook?
Will he make many supplications to you?
Will he speak softly to you?
[Aggressive]
Will he make a covenant with you?
[Unfaithful or disloyal]
Will you take him as a servant forever?
[Not a servant]
Will you play with him as with a bird,
[Wild]
Or will you leash him for your maidens?
[Doesn't submit]
Will your companions make a banquet of him?
[Wants to be served]
Will they apportion him among the merchants?
Can you fill his skin with harpoons,
Or his head with fishing spears?
Lay your hand on him;
[Fights]
Remember the battle—
[Quarreling personality]
Never do it again!
Indeed, any hope of overcoming him is false;
[Without God you cannot overcome this]

Shall one not be overwhelmed at the sight of him?
[Tries to steal God's glory]
No one is so fierce that he would dare stir him up.
[Don't poke or trigger this personality]
Who then is able to stand against Me?
Who has preceded Me, that I should pay him?
Everything under heaven is Mine.

I will not conceal his limbs,
His mighty power, or his graceful proportions.
[Intimidating]
Who can remove his outer coat?
[Hard to penetrate]
Who can approach him with a double bridle?
[Unapproachable]
Who can open the doors of his face,
With his terrible teeth all around?
His rows of scales are his pride,
[Prideful and boastful]
Shut up tightly as with a seal;
One is so near another
That no air can come between them;
[No air, no wind, no Holy Spirit]
They are joined one to another,
They stick together and cannot be parted.
His sneezings flash forth light,
And his eyes are like the eyelids of the morning.
Out of his mouth go burning lights;
[His words are deadly]
Sparks of fire shoot out.

[Like fiery arrows or fiery darts]

Smoke goes out of his nostrils,

[Prideful anger]

As from a boiling pot and burning rushes.

[Hot tempered]

His breath kindles coals,

And a flame goes out of his mouth.

Strength dwells in his neck,

[Stiff-necked, unteachable]

And sorrow dances before him.

[Causes spirit of sadness]

The folds of his flesh are joined together;

They are firm on him and cannot be moved.

His heart is as hard as stone,

[Lack of compassion and understanding]

Even as hard as the lower millstone.

When he raises himself up, the mighty are afraid;

[Operates through fear]

Because of his crashings they are beside themselves.

Though the sword reaches him, it cannot avail;

Nor does spear, dart, or javelin.

[Nothing penetrates]

He regards iron as straw,

And bronze as rotten wood.

The arrow cannot make him flee;

Slingstones become like stubble to him.

Darts are regarded as straw;

He laughs at the threat of javelins.

His undersides are like sharp potsherds;

He spreads pointed marks in the mire.
He makes the deep boil like a pot;
He makes the sea like a pot of ointment.
He leaves a shining wake behind him;
One would think the deep had white hair.
On earth there is nothing like him,
Which is made without fear.
He beholds every high thing;
He is king over all the children of pride (Job 41 NKJV).

If there is any gambling history in your family, you need to break generational curses and close open doors to kick out Leviathan. If you are not giving your tithes and offerings as your first priority, then you have an open door and a curse in your life.

"Will a mere mortal rob God? Yet you rob me. But you ask, 'How are we robbing you?' In tithes and offerings. You are under a curse—your whole nation—because you are robbing me. Bring the whole tithe into the storehouse, that there may be food in my house. Test me in this," says the Lord Almighty, "and see if I will not throw open the floodgates of heaven and pour out so much blessing that there will not be room enough to store it. I will prevent pests from devouring your crops, and the vines in your fields will not drop their fruit before it is ripe," says the Lord Almighty. "Then all the nations will call you blessed, for yours will be a delightful land," says the Lord Almighty (Malachi 3:8-12).

How to Get Rid of Leviathan

Humble yourself, repent, and renounce your pride and your attempts to steal God's glory in any way or form. Then, cut all your generational ties with your ancestors to destroy the Leviathan in your life, in Jesus Christ's Name. Amen.

1. Humble yourself. You must first crucify your pride to be free from Leviathan.

2. Repent from pride, entitlement, stealing God's glory and His tithes and offerings. Repent from any idol worship and renounce your gods one by one, including yourself. Self-pity is idol worship.

3. Repent, one by one, from any other characteristics of the Leviathan listed earlier.

4. If the Leviathan came into your personality through your ancestors, break every attachment in the Name of Jesus Christ. Renounce and expel lack, debt, famine, barrenness, and drought from your life and your family in Jesus' Name!

5. Bind the spirit of Leviathan and cast it out in Jesus Christ's Name.

6. Loose the Holy Spirit's blessings and freedom from lack, debt, failure, and poverty.

7. Declare the power of the blood of Jesus Christ over you. Glorify Jesus, declaring His goodness and attributes.

8. Remove all generational curses of lack, failure, debt, and poverty with a prayer. Seek the Holy Spirit and reflect on your ancestors' histories, where Leviathan might have entered in. Then, uproot this spirit from your life and the lives of your family with a prayer. You must command this spirit to leave,

and you need to mean it to kick the enemy out of your life and your blessings.

9. Declare God's provision and prosperity over your life.

10. Giving thanks to God multiplies your blessings.

11. Ask for the divine wisdom of God to handle your blessings and be a good steward.

12. Also, treating the person who has a Leviathan spirit with *agape* love is a winning strategy.

Judas

This is a betraying, deceiving, lying, and greedy spirit. This spirit will seek to be near the leader of any ministry or organization. This spirit goes hand in hand with the Python spirit that is depressed and suicidal. Pride is an open door to Judas.

This spirit brings entitlement to steal from anyone's time, money, resources, friends, and more. It is a jealous spirit. You need discernment to cast this spirit out of your life, ministry, family, and workplace.

My family and I opened our doors to a young girl who, little by little, secretly poisoned our teenage daughter to rebel against my husband and me. She told her terrible things about us that damaged our daughter deeply. She secretly brought pornography and lust into our house and defiled our home. Thankfully, God exposed this spirit and she confessed her wrongdoing, including wrecking the marriage of our dear friends. Be very careful who you bring into your life and household. She confessed that she was also jealous over her best friend's marriage and put a curse on her marriage, coveting her husband. She said she had many snakes and devils in her and admitted that she was hateful.

Characteristics of a Judas Spirit

- This spirit operates through lies and deception.
- It always judges and undermines authority.
- Their repentance is not true repentance, just like in the example of Judas; it only knows remorse. People may cry and weep in front of you, but it doesn't mean they are repenting sincerely. Emotional expressions don't always confirm the truthfulness of the heart.
- Many religious Pharisees who think they know the truth but only have religion are operating under this spirit.
- A suicidal spirit is behind it.
- It operates through a murderous spirit.
- It betrays and sells out easily.
- It is an accusing spirit.

Spirit of Rebellion

This demonic stronghold is a major open door to demons of Jezebel and Leviathan. The Bible states that the spirit of rebellion is equal to witchcraft. Rebellion can display itself in different ways and forms. If a person has an issue with submitting to authority, management, leaders, pastors, parents, government, and even to husband or wife, it is an opening for the spirit of rebellion to enter in, and this demon is a door-opener to other demons.

The spirit of rebellion hinders our obedience to the leading of the Holy Spirit. I have seen many churches and ministries divided because of the power struggles and pride that opened the door to the demon of rebellion. This demon speaks to your pride, your rights, and your self-indulgence in order to justify why you are in the right, why the other person is in the wrong, and why you should not submit.

People who have a rebellious spirit are always sick and tired, because rebellious demons who open the door to the spirit of witchcraft bring sickness, depression, and fatigue. These people's ears are not sensitive to the voice of the Holy Spirit. They will always justify why they are not in submission. Many churches are unable to grow because of the rebellious spirit of pastors' wives who are not in alignment with their husbands' leadership and who despise their authority.

Spirit of Mockery

This demon accompanies the spirit of rebellion. When the mind operates in the natural and intellectual realms to the extent of rejecting the supernatural power of God and the presence of the Holy Spirit, we see the spirit of mockery on display.

Once I was called up by a spiritual leader to pray with someone for deliverance. During the deliverance prayer, the spiritual leader started cracking up jokes and making carnal comments that completely distracted me and the person I was praying with. Her irreverent behavior to the Holy Spirit nullified the effect of our prayers. I felt like I had wasted my time by accepting her invitation for help. Later on, I saw the same person chatting and laughing with people when they were responding to the altar call and pouring out their hearts in anguish. She would interrupt their encounter with the Holy Spirit and start chatting with them while they were at the altar expecting deliverance and breakthrough. This is a mocking spirit. Psalm 1 talks about the mockers. These types of personalities are mostly people who have been hurt by the church in their past and stop taking church seriously, which subconsciously includes the move of the Holy Spirit.

Spirit of Accusation

The devil is called the accuser of the brethren. He accuses us day and night, the Scripture says, according to Revelation 12:10-11. The accusing demon comes directly from the Antichrist spirit to bring accusation, guilt, and condemnation. Many abuse victims—people who were rejected, neglected, and abandoned in childhood, who have an "orphan spirit"—are open prey to this demon. They continuously accuse and condemn others. They feel everyone owes them something because of the tragedies they endured in their childhood.

People in church with this demon will constantly accuse the pastor, other believers, and even the entire church. It is a victim mentality that accuses others for not meeting their needs, and is a self-seeking, attention-seeking spirit that makes everyone owe them something. This spirit opens a wider door to the spirit of Python.

Short List of Common Accusation Bondages

- All addictions
- Irrational reactions/attitudes
- Suicidal thoughts, death
- Depression
- Impulsive/addictive behaviors
- Anger
- Rage

- Accusation, slander, and strife
- Victim mentality, self-pity
- Attention addiction
- Emotional eating and gluttony
- Insecurities
- Inferiority
- Fear and anxiety
- Unforgiveness, bitterness, and revenge
- Cruelty, meanness, and rudeness
- Hysterical crying episodes
- Tormented thinking
- Nightmares and demonic visions
- Constant guilt, shame, and condemnation
- Addiction to negative talk or pessimism
- Lies and deception
- Lust, perversion, and whoredom

Drama Addiction Is Demonic

Jezebel and Leviathan

Drama addiction is demonic and operates under the Leviathan and Jezebel duo. It robs people of their talents, gifts, families, friends, finances, energy, time, life, potential, promotion, and destiny.

For though we walk in the flesh, we do not war according to the flesh. For the weapons of our warfare are not carnal but mighty *in God for pulling down strongholds, casting down arguments and **every high thing that exalts itself against the knowledge of God**, bringing every thought into captivity to the obedience of Christ, and being ready to punish all disobedience when your obedience is fulfilled* (2 Corinthians 10:3-6 NKJV).

I would like to bring to your attention the phrase *"every high thing that exalts itself against the knowledge of God"* in this passage. The drama queen sets herself up high and exalts herself by trying to get all the attention and taking the attention from Jesus Christ. That is a demonic attachment behind the scenes, blended with a victim mentality.

The simplest way to characterize this toxic demonic behavior is that it's excessive attention-seeking that is lodged in a soul deeply wounded during childhood by rejection, abandonment, or neglect. Beneath it is an unnourished, extreme desperation for love.

We all come across people who are prone to, or a magnet for, drama. Maybe this is you, but until now you were not aware of it. For some reason, you cause or attract drama. This can be especially true if you've come from a dysfunctional home, rejected by your parents and/or siblings, and you're craving attention. Subconsciously, the only way a drama queen or king can get attention is to create some sort of negative situation with a storyline around unfair treatment she or he is facing.

At one time in my life I had to be around someone like this. She was always suspicious, paranoid, and thinking malicious thoughts about people's motives. She was crying to me all the time and was believing in her own lies. One day I realized her lie world was her reality, and it wasn't possible to convince her without the Holy Spirit giving her that revelation. She was blaming people who were helping her, believing they were out to get her or talking behind her back. She needed constant recognition and attention to feel important, otherwise she would create the drama. When the owner of the company or important guests visited, she made sure her laughter was louder, her reactions were excessive, and she pointed all the conversations toward herself.

Because drama does get attention temporarily, this compulsive behavior personality gets satisfaction for a short season, then finds another point of origin to start a new drama. This is very similar to a drug addiction.

As mentioned earlier, the drama addiction operates under two demons—the Jezebel spirit, which is the controlling, pushy, false prophetess with uncontrollable power cravings; and the Leviathan spirit, who twists other people's words and actions and causes lack, debt, financial struggles, and an unfulfilled life and potential. I sought the Holy Spirit, the Spirit of Truth, on this subject for a while in prayer. The revelation I got was simpler than I thought. First, the Holy Spirit answered me with a question: "Why do you think that a person cannot have both Jezebel and Leviathan demons, since in My Word, Mark 5, he can have legions?" That was an eye-opener question. The drama queen operates under both Jezebel and Leviathan demons.

Recognize the drama trap and run away!

Drama addiction, as mentioned earlier, is rooted in self-pity, an inferiority complex, and the victim mentality. It is a sign of a severely damaged and toxic personality due to abandonment and rejection. Rejection in childhood is the main cause of it. This demonic force causes constant *accusations*. It is fed by *attention* and operates with *blame games*. Something has always been done wrong to a drama queen, and she constantly accuses. This spirit is under Leviathan's major power, and the symptoms manifest as an emotional, physical, financial, and spiritual roller coaster. Don't join any accusations or slanders of a drama queen.

The Bible says, "The devil is the *accuser* of the brethren." It's a slanderous, restless spirit, and it gossips in a crafty way. It's a toxic personality and hurts families, friendships, and ministries. Don't give an ear to drama or self-pity talk. You must set boundaries with drama-addicted people. Those who have this demon are stuck in life and don't go far, even though they may have so many gifts and talents. But because they're a magnet for drama, they instantly blow great opportunities by magnifying issues. It's a control- and attention-seeking spirit. Run away from drama queens and drama addicts! It's a trap! It will suck you up like a vacuum if you pay it any attention!

Low self-esteem and a poor self-image also cause an addiction to approval and attention and do not arise from a true identity or self-worth.

Characteristics of a Drama Queen: Jezebel and Leviathan Combo

- Becomes upset unless they are the center of attention, especially if someone else is the center of success and attention
- Argumentative
- In denial—the problem is always elsewhere
- Creating chaos and turmoil
- Can't relax and rest, repeats the matter, cannot let go
- Falling madly in love and in hate when their ego isn't fed
- Self-destructive and distractive personality
- Shielded with her own truths and facts, which are lies

- Rapidly shifting emotions, impulsive and extreme mood swings—one day mountaintop experience and the next day in the deepest pit
- Acts very dramatically and theatrically, as if in front of an audience
- Exaggerates emotions and expressions while being insincere
- Concerned and sad with her physical appearance
- Constantly seeking reassurance, praise, reward, encouragement, and approval
- Easily influenced by the words, news, or comments of others
- Extremely sensitive to criticism and defensive when corrected
- Feels unappreciated and not recognized
- Low tolerance for frustration
- Has trouble focusing, starting and completing assignments
- Highly sensitive—reacts with great emotions
- Always the victim, believes some people are purposely after them to do them harm
- Suspicious and paranoid behavior rooted in fear and insecurities
- Self-centered, self-advertising, and self-glory-seeking, even though demonstrating concern for others
- Has short-term and not lasting relationships
- Cannot get ignored or not acknowledged, but must be recognized and acknowledged
- Threatens getting sick or even suicidal to get attention
- Passive-aggressive behavior

- Stirring up problems and turning small things into mountains

Why do you bring drama queens into your life?

I asked this question many times, until one day I directly asked the only true source, the Holy Spirit. I prayed, "Holy Spirit, Spirit of Truth, please reveal to me—why am I often attracting drama queens to my life? In Jesus Christ's Name, amen."

Whenever I have prayed this prayer, without exception, the Holy Spirit has given me a revelation. He gently whispered to my heart, "Your mother was a drama queen, and all your childhood you tried to cure her, fix her, and make her happy. This is your familiar spirit. Because of your mother, you have false compassion to this personality. Break your soul ties and your commitment to giving your devotion to this spirit." And I did. The freedom and joy were amazing.

How to Break Drama Addiction

If you have this type of personality, know that the enemy is stealing your potential, your time, your promotion, finances, health, relationships, and your blessings. When you are set free from this bondage, your life will change for the better and you will prosper.

1. Recognize your drama addiction.
2. Humble yourself and confess.
3. Renounce this spirit and repent for your agreement with it.
4. Ask Jesus to heal your soul wounds—rejection, neglect, abandonment, inferiority, self-hatred, low self-esteem, poor

self-image, etc. List them one by one. Pray and receive the restoration of your soul.

5. Purposefully continue choosing to live a low-key, relaxed life, seeking no credit or attention. Get over yourself!

Powerful Tips

✤ *Praying the Word of God is praying the will of God.*

✤ *You are the landlord of your life, body, soul, and destiny. Evict the enemy! Don't be timid about evicting the devil.*

✤ *You don't ask the demons to leave you. You don't request evil spirits to go away. You command them and cast them out. You have the authority of Jesus Christ. Mean business and never give up. The enemy must know you are serious about kicking him out.*

Chapter 7

THREE THINGS *You* MUST KNOW BEFORE *Your* DELIVERANCE

As you probably know by now, deliverance is not an undertaking to jump into completely blind. The seven sons of Sceva learned that lesson the hard way (see Acts 19). They thought they'd just copy what they saw other people doing and the demons would leave. Unfortunately for them, the demons didn't leave; they turned on the sons of Sceva and beat them up! These would-be deliverance ministers didn't know the three basic things necessary for successful deliverance. These are:

1. Know your God
2. Know yourself and your identity
3. Know your enemy

1. Know Your God

You must know your God to be able to trust Him, His love, His goodness, His Word, His promises, and His power to deliver you. Without knowing your God, your true, living Redeemer, it is impossible for you to be delivered from any demonic oppression or possession.

The true God, the Creator of the Universe and everything in it, has a name. Children of God, Christians, don't worship the gods of any other religion. Our God has a name.

In Exodus 3, Moses asked God His name, which was a very wise question. God answered Moses:

> *God said to Moses, "I am who I am. This is what you are to say to the Israelites: 'I am has sent me to you.'" God also said to Moses, "Say to the Israelites, 'The Lord, the God of your fathers—the God of Abraham, the God of Isaac and the God of Jacob—has sent me to you.'* **This is my name forever, the name you shall call me from generation to generation"** (Exodus 3:14-15).

The Hebrew word for "God" is *elohim*. But even for the false gods such as Baal, people used the word *elohim*. This is the very reason the word begins with a small letter, because it is not a name. Just as anyone can call anything their god, the word *god* does not mean the Creator, the true God, but His Name does. Don't you want to be called by your name?

But when it came to the true God, He was called *El Elohim Israel*, which is "God of Israel." But this is still *not* the exact name of God that God gave Moses as His Name. Instead, He said, "I am the Lord God of Abraham, God of Isaac, and God of Jacob."

I AM: Now, in Hebrew, "I AM" is a name, and comes from the word *hayah*, which means Self-Existing One or *be*. Therefore, it is not as in English, where we are talking about "I am" in the present tense; *I AM* means forever and ever.

Lord: "Lord" is not a word as in *lord*, but it is a Name—Yehovah (also Yahweh), which is the national name for the God of Israel (or *El Elohim Israel*).

When Jesus said in John 8:58, "Before Abraham was born, I am!" He was declaring that He was (and He is) the Yehovah (Yahweh).

The Jews wanted to kill Him for this declaration, because one of the Ten Commandments is "Do not use the Name of the Lord thy God in vain." Even God's own people, out of fear, were not using God's Name. And now, imagine Jesus declaring Himself as Yahweh.

At this point we must know that Jesus (whose name means "Yehovah is salvation") comes from the Hebrew *Yehowshuwa*, the root of which is Yehovah and comes from the root word *hayah*—"Self-Existing One, Be, I AM."

Is the True, Living God Your God?

Jesus Christ came down to earth, God in human form, to show us God's love and redemptive power for the entirety of mankind. He died on the cross for our sins and rose from the dead on the third day. He is the Son of the living God. It is through His sonship that we can be God's children—sons and daughters.

There is no other way to heaven than through Jesus (see John 14:6). Anyone who invites Jesus into her/his heart becomes a child of God (see John 1:12; Gal. 3:26).

Triune God in Three Persons—Father, Son, and Holy Spirit

The Lord God, Creator of everything, is One in three persons. God created us in His own image; therefore we are also triune in nature, and we have a body, soul, and spirit.

How Do You Receive Jesus Christ as Your Lord and Savior?

If you want to receive Jesus Christ into your heart as your Lord and Savior, pray the following prayer. (You can pray in your own words. The most important thing is that you truly believe when you pray.)

Dear Lord Jesus,

I believe that You are the Son of the Living God and the only way to heaven. I believe that You died on the cross for my sins and rose from the dead on the third day and conquered death. Please forgive my sins and be the Lord of my heart and life. Amen.

If you prayed this prayer, you are a child of God and saved from eternal punishment, which is hell. You belong to God and God's family. I suggest that every time you go through a spiritual attack, you declare Jesus as your Lord and Savior and yourself as a child of God out loud.

Believe, Praise, and Declare

Lord God, You are good; Your love and mercies endure forever (Psalm 136, Psalm 118, Psalm 107).

Lord God, You are kind (Psalm 145).

Lord God, You are Love (1 John 4:8).

You are my Rock, my Deliverer (Psalm 144).

You are Most High (Psalm 91).

You are my Shepherd (Psalm 23).

You are my Refuge and Fortress; I trust You (Psalm 91).

God, You are my strength (Psalm 81).

God, You are near (Psalm 75).

Lord God, You are my Redeemer (Job 19:25).

Lord, You are my Rock and my Salvation (Psalm 62:6).

You are the God of Justice (Psalm 50:6).

Lord God, You are Most High and awesome; You are the great King over all the earth (Psalm 47:2).

You are my Refuge and Strength, an ever-present help in trouble (Psalm 46).

You are God, my joy and delight (Psalm 43:4).

Lord God, You are my Light and my Salvation and the stronghold of my life (Psalm 27:1).

Lord God, the earth is Yours and everything in it (Psalm 24).

Lord God, You are the King of glory (Psalm 24:7).

Lord God, I love You, my strength, my rock, my fortress, and my deliverer; You are my rock and refuge, my shield and the horn of my salvation and my stronghold (Psalm 18:1-2).

Lord, You alone are my portion and my cup; You make my lot secure (Psalm 16:5).

You are my Creator (Ecclesiastes 12:1).

You are my Wonderful Counselor, Everlasting Father, Mighty God, Prince of Peace (Isaiah 9:6).

Lord God, You are my defense (Isaiah 12:2).

You are the Holy One of Israel (Isaiah 12:6).

You are the Righteous One (Isaiah 24:16).

You are the Alpha and Omega (Revelation 1:8).

You are King of kings and Lord of lords (Revelation 19:16).

You are the First and the Last, the Beginning and the End (Revelation 22:13).

Lord God, You are my Redeemer (Isaiah 43:14, Isaiah 44:6).

Lord God, You are the Way, the Truth, and the Life (John 14:6).

You are the good Shepherd (John 10:11).

You are the Gate (John 10:7).

You are the Resurrection and the Life (John 11:25).

You are the Bread of Life (John 6:35).

You are the Light of the world (John 8:12).

You are my Advocate (John 15:26).

You are the vine, I am the branch (John 15:5).

You are my Friend (John 15:15).

You are my High Priest (Hebrews 4:14-16, Hebrews 5:5,6).

You are the Word (John 1).

There are so many more Scriptures to exalt our God. But for now, I am sharing these with you to start declaring and praising God with these to win your battles and live a victorious life.

2. Know Yourself and Your Identity

Power of Your Identity

Over the last few years, I have met many people who are in identity crises. They may think they know who they are, but it is not their true identity. They have accepted a false identity that leaves them feeling insecure. Those who know their true identity are strong and certain of who they are in Jesus Christ.

I myself struggled for so many years with my identity. I had to allow Holy Spirit to reveal to me my true identity. I believed in such lies about myself for so many years and I ended up not knowing who I was. This is why I am passionate about helping people find and embrace their true identity. Society always tries to have a say in who we are. The truth is your identity doesn't come from your last name, your friend group, your biology (skin color, shape, size, health, etc.), society, and even culture, but it comes from God, the One who created *you!*

The main issue that we are dealing with in this generation is an identity crisis. People are starting to question who they are and change themselves into something else, something they simply are not. I challenge you to read the first three chapters of Genesis. There you will see the vital foundation for everything we believe in as Christians. I also encourage you to read the Word of God more; the more you know God the more you will know yourself.

If I made a dish and gave it to you, you wouldn't ask someone else what was in it or how he made it. You would ask me those questions because I was the one who made it. You wouldn't ask anyone else because they wouldn't know. In the same way, we should be going directly to the One who created us to fully know who we are.

I always wanted to be someone else. I have a friend who is a very sweet person. Her voice is seriously like the voice of an angel. I tried to talk like her once. I even prayed to God to make me like her. Jesus said to me, "If you become like her, you'll get nothing done. I called you to be you to accomplish the great task that's in front of you."

Many people try to live like someone else. They don't know what kind of power they would have if they lived in perfect peace and alignment with their identity.

You're a masterpiece, but you probably don't know it.

You're special, but most likely you don't feel it.

You're beautiful, but you think something has to be fixed about your appearance for you to look beautiful.

You're smart, but there is a very high chance that others made you believe you're not.

Maybe you don't like yourself.

You may think you can't love yourself.

Your failures and mistakes might be magnified and become a torment.

You may be rejected and feeling less than everyone around you.

They put many labels on you and you bought them. You owned them and you believed in them.

You may be abused, molested, raped, used, divorced, bankrupted, betrayed, rejected, abandoned, neglected, unloved, bullied, unfulfilled, and ridiculed. You don't know who you are anymore. You're feeling lost. You're running away from your past. You're running away from God. You're running away from facing the truth. You're running away from your enemies. This is exhausting. Who are you really? What's your purpose in life? What's your identity?

There's a book for you in heaven!

Insecurity

Insecurity can ruin your life. Insecurity comes from not knowing and embracing who we are but comparing ourselves with others. "If I just accomplish this, I will be worthy. If I make a certain income, I will feel better about myself. If my hair was curly and blonde or straight and dark... If my eye color was green or blue... If I just could play a piano or a guitar...."

The world is throwing its own standards at us through media, and unfortunately we're buying it. If you're trying really hard to do something and expending a lot of effort for your goal, there is always a reason why! There's a statistic that short men in America usually drive big trucks; overweight women spend more money on clothing than food; people who believe they are average looking or not good looking focus on a higher level of education. These people are insecure about their perceived defects, so they are trying to make up for it in oher ways.

I grew up being sick all the time. My mother and my grandmother were both hypochondriacs—they had an abnormal anxiety about health and many unwarranted fears about serious diseases. Growing up in a house like that, I wasn't allowed to run or sweat, and I would go out very rarely. Most of the time I watched other kids playing through the window. I was always jealous of the athletic girls who were good at sports. If I was ever out, no one wanted me on their team. I was the weakest one. When I grew up, I tried so hard to compensate for it by playing sports and exercising.

Are you trying to compensate for what hurt your self-worth or identity?

I counseled several Chinese women in the past. In China, daughters are often considered undesirable. All of these women felt like they had to work harder than their husbands and make more money to compensate for their low self-worth as women. They had disappointed their families by being born female, so they tried to compensate by proving that they could be "even better" than a man. What your family values will become your own set of values and later your identity.

Are you trying to compensate? Are you comparing yourself? Are you believing in a lie?

Knowing Who You Are Changes Everything

Years ago after I preached at a conference on freedom from insecurities, a man came to me in tears. As he spoke, he broke down and started weeping with such agony and grief that it was hard to understand what he was saying. He told me he was a doctor. He said that when he was young, he knew he was called into humanitarian work to help people in the most unfortunate places. He had such passion for it that it was like a fire in his bones.

But he was a short guy, and he was insecure about it. His family always said that being a doctor meant you had arrived in life. A doctor was the highest place in society, the greatest achievement. Listen to me—being a doctor is a noble and a great profession, but nothing can ever be better than what God has called you to be.

This man said to himself that if he just could become a doctor, he could be higher than anyone. So instead of going after his dream, he went to the medical school and became a doctor. He told me that he now has everything in materialistic ways, but he has never been happy or fulfilled. The good news is, he has learned how to find freedom from his insecurities! He is now going on mission trips.

It is crazy how we compensate for our brokenness by unconsciously coming up with unhealthy solutions in our brains rather than embracing our identity. How differently would we approach life if we saw ourselves as God sees us?

Your Identity in Christ

Your God-given identity has power. It's powerful to know who you are and what you supposed to do with your life.

Are you walking in the right identity? Maybe your family, friends, society, culture, or others labeled you and gave you an identity that is not the one God has for you. Maybe you know yourself through the eyes of other people or what you do/have done instead of through the eyes of grace.

If you have experienced bullying, intimidation, abuse, molestation, rape, rejection, neglect, or abandonment, you may have a false identity. People and events do not label you. Your past has no authority over your future. Only knowing who you are in Christ matters, and when you establish that, God will change your destiny.

Begin to read and meditate on the truths of God's Word and His identity for you. (I will share many of these truths below, if you don't know where to start.) God wants you to know how important and loved you are in Him today.

How Do I Know I'm Living by a False Identity?

Are you living by the identity the world has given you? Are you believing the lies of the enemy that have been spoken over your life? If what you've been told does not match with who God says you are—what He has said about you in His living Word—then what you're living by is a false identity.

Do you feel insecure? Are you looking for "love" in others—in a girlfriend, a boyfriend, a spouse, or your children? Do you get comfort and security from the job title you have, the amount of income you make, or with your material possessions? Identifying with worldly things—anything outside of the Word of God—is a false identity. God's Word is truth, and He loves you so much that through Christ you have been given authority and identity.

Stop! Stop believing in the lies told about who you are. You are not stupid, ugly, too silly to be taken seriously, weak, small, unimportant, etc. I am here to tell you today that God wants you to know who you truly are to Him because His opinion is *fact*—it is the *truth*. Everything that God says should be the only thing that matters. You need to set aside your insecurities and embrace the reality of who you are in Christ—loved, accepted, victorious, single-minded, strong, important, and a world changer! Knowing who you are in Christ is knowing your identity!

What went wrong? Why do we struggle to resemble God, which is our true identity? (See Genesis 1:27.) Part of being made in God's image is that Adam and Eve had the ability to make free choices. Although they were given a righteous nature, they made an evil choice to rebel against God. The result of this was separation; they disfigured the image of God within themselves and passed that damaged likeness down (see Rom. 5:12). Today, we still bear the image of God, but we also bear the scars of sin. Mentally, morally, socially, and physically, we show the effects of sin.

But there is good news! When someone gets saved, God begins to restore His original image back to them, creating a "new self, created to be like God in true righteousness and holiness" (Eph. 4:24). That redemption happens only by God's grace through faith in Jesus Christ as our Savior from the sin that separates us from God (see Eph. 2:8-9). Through Christ, we are made new creations in the likeness of God (see 2 Cor. 5:17).

When you identify with Christ, God gives you a new identity.

- Instead of sinner, you are called saint.
- Instead of lost, you are called found.
- Instead of enemy, you are called friend.
- Instead of unrighteous, you are called righteous.

- Instead of sick, you are called healed.
- Instead of poor, you are called rich.

Prayer

Heavenly Father, I come before You willing to walk in my true identity as Your child. I am sorry for believing lies about myself. Help me see myself the way You see me. It is You who created me and my identity is in You. Thank You for Your sovereignty and goodness. Guide me in Your ways and give me a hunger to seek You more. In Jesus' Name, Amen.

Receiving Your Identity in Christ

The world has an effect on our identities as well. People have been speaking over you your whole life, and if you allow it, it will become who you are. Instead of asking the question, "Who am I?" you need to ask yourself, "*Whose* am I?" Are you the world's? Are you God's? Or, maybe, are you your own god?

When you are going through life and nothing is challenging you at all, you're probably not walking in your true identity as a child of God.

> *If the world hates you, keep in mind that it hated me first. If you belonged to the world, it would love you as its own. As it is, you do not belong to the world, but I have chosen you out of the world. That is why the world hates you* (John 15:18-19).

This week I was praying on this topic of identity, and I was reminded of the uniqueness of mankind. There is nothing like us on earth. We were created in God's image. The Creator of the whole universe created us in

His image, His likeness. Having the "image" or "likeness" of God means that we were made to resemble God. For instance, we have the ability to reason and choose; this is a reflection of God's freedom and wisdom. Humanity was originally created in righteousness and perfect innocence; this is a reflection of God's holiness. We were created for fellowship—a reflection of God's love and true nature.

You were made in His image, so do you look like Him? What you do flows from who you are. I believe that we must be constantly growing. God didn't create us to be robots; He wants us to do things out of desire. Not because He told us to but because we want to love Him, praise Him, and testify to His goodness. God is so worthy of your praise and of your life, because He created you!

When you know your identity, you know your purpose! When you know who you are, you know where you're going. It's amazing how these two things work together.

You might be reading this and feeling like you're not walking out your true identity as a child of God. You feel stuck in this continual cycle of sin; nothing is really changing in your life or in your heart (I've been there, I understand). For something to new to begin, something old has to die. In order to walk in your true identity, you must surrender your old self to God. By doing so you give Him access to mold your heart into His. This should be our desire—to have hearts like God. It all comes down to you making a choice. You must choose an identity and walk in it.

Dear Lord Jesus,

Thank You for saving me! Thank You for seating me on high in heavenly realms with You. Thank You for making me a Child of the Most High God. I am not forsaken or abandoned but deeply loved by my Father who loves me and formed me in my mother's womb. I have been predestined to be adopted into sonship through Christ, and I receive this identity now.

Forgive me for letting the lies of the enemy define me. I am not what the world says I am, but I am who Your Word has called me to be. I am a beloved son/daughter of the great I AM. I bind all future lies of the enemy and humbly accept my title to sonship through Christ today. Thank You, Jesus. May I humbly live my life for You, in Your love, mercy, and grace. In Jesus' mighty Name, amen.

God's Word on Your Identity

You're Created in God's Own Image

So God created mankind in his own image, in the image of God he created them; male and female he created them (Genesis 1:27).

You're created in God's own image. That means you're the greatest masterpiece God has created. You're brilliant, beautiful, and gifted. If you invited Jesus into your heart as your Lord and Savior, here is a list of some of the attributes of your identity:

You're a Child of God!

Yet to all who did receive him, to those who believed in his name, he gave the right to become children of God (John 1:12).

So you are no longer a slave, but God's child; and since you are his child, God has made you also an heir (Galatians 4:7).

He predestined us for adoption to sonship through Jesus Christ, in accordance with his pleasure and will—to the praise of his glorious grace, which he has freely given us in the One he loves (Ephesians 1:5-6).

Because you are his sons [and daughters], *God sent the Spirit of his Son into our hearts, the Spirit who calls out, "Abba, Father." So you are no longer a slave, but God's child; and since you are his child, God has made you also an heir* (Galatians 4:6-7).

See what great love the Father has lavished on us, that we should be called children of God! And that is what we are! The reason the world does not know us is that it did not know him. Dear friends, now we are children of God, and what we will be has not yet been made known. But we know that when Christ appears, we shall be like him, for we shall see him as he is (1 John 3:1-2).

So in Christ Jesus you are all children of God through faith, for all of you who were baptized into Christ have clothed yourselves with Christ. There is neither Jew nor Gentile, neither slave nor free, nor is there male and female, for you are all one in Christ Jesus. If you belong to Christ, then you are Abraham's seed, and heirs according to the promise (Galatians 3:26-29).

Now you, brothers and sisters, like Isaac, are children of promise. At that time the son born according to the flesh persecuted the son born by the power of the Spirit. It is the same now (Galatians 4:28-29).

Understand, then, that those who have faith are children of Abraham. Scripture foresaw that God would justify the Gentiles by faith, and announced the gospel in advance to Abraham: "All nations will be blessed through you." So those who rely on faith are blessed along with Abraham, the man of faith (Galatians 3:7-9).

You Are Loved

*As the Father has loved Me, so have **I loved you. Abide in My love.** If you keep My commandments, you will abide **in My love,** just as I have kept My Father's commandments and **abide in His love*** (John 15:9-10 NKJV).

You are loved by God more than you could possibly imagine. His eyes are always upon you (see Isa. 49:16). He knows the exact number of days of your life (see Ps. 139:16). He numbers the hairs on your head (see Luke 12:7). He saves each of your tears (see Ps. 56:8). You are deeply, deeply loved by God.

God shows his love *for us in that while we were still sinners, Christ died for us* (Romans 5:8 ESV).

*Through him we have also obtained access by faith into this grace in which we stand, and we rejoice in hope of the glory of God. Not only that, but we rejoice in our sufferings, knowing that suffering produces endurance, and endurance produces character, and character produces hope, and hope does not put us to shame, because **God's love has been poured into our hearts** through the Holy Spirit who has been given to us* (Romans 5:2-5 ESV).

*But God, being rich in mercy, **because of the great love with which he loved us,** even when we were dead in our trespasses, made us alive together with Christ—by grace you have been saved* (Ephesians 2:4-5 ESV).

*See what kind of **love the Father has given to us**, that we should be called children of God; and so we are. The reason why the world does not know us is that it did not know him* (1 John 3:1 ESV).

Beloved, let us love one another, for love is from God, and whoever loves has been born of God and knows God. Anyone who does not love does not know God, because God is love (1 John 4:7-8 ESV).

You're a New Creation

If anyone is in Christ, he is a new creation; old things have passed away; behold, all things have become new (2 Corinthians 5:17 NKJV).

For we are God's handiwork, created in Christ Jesus to do good works, which God prepared in advance for us to do (Ephesians 2:10).

You're Accepted

Accept one another, then, just as Christ accepted you, in order to bring praise to God (Romans 15:7).

Many people suffer with the scars of rejection. Abandonment and neglect can cause wounds of rejection. When we're rejected, we perceive ourselves as worthless. We're not good enough.

You are accepted. Even if you feel like you never really fit in, you aren't part of the inner circle at work, or you have a hard time connecting with others—God accepts you. With all of your ways and quirks, you're in with the One who made the universe. You are His beloved child.

You're Called by God

You're called to be a worshiper. You're called to be have a fellowship with God. You're called to serve God. You're called to increase.

Before I formed you in the womb I knew you, before you were born I set you apart; I appointed you as a prophet to the nations (Jeremiah 1:5).

You're Beautiful

For you created my inmost being; you knit me together in my mother's womb. I praise you because I am fearfully and wonderfully made; your works are wonderful (Psalm 139:13-14).

You're Set Free

It is for freedom that Christ has set us free. Stand firm, then, and do not let yourselves be burdened again by a yoke of slavery (Galatians 5:1).

You, my brothers and sisters, were called to be free (Galatians 5:13).

You're the Righteousness of God

God made him who had no sin to be sin for us, so that in him we might become the righteousness of God (2 Corinthians 5:21).

You're Healed

"He himself bore our sins" in his body on the cross, so that we might die to sins and live for righteousness; "by his wounds you have been healed" (1 Peter 2:24).

You're One with Christ

For all of you who were baptized into Christ have clothed yourselves with Christ. There is neither Jew nor Gentile, neither slave nor free, nor is there male and female, for you are all one in Christ Jesus (Galatians 3:27-28).

Since, then, you have been raised with Christ, set your hearts on things above, where Christ is, seated at the right hand of God. Set your minds on things above, not on earthly things. For you died, and your life is now hidden with Christ in God (Colossians 3:1-3).

But now in Christ Jesus you who once were far away have been brought near by the blood of Christ (Ephesians 2:13).

God raised us up with Christ and seated us with him in the heavenly realms in Christ Jesus (Ephesians 2:6).

Because of his great love for us, God, who is rich in mercy, made us alive with Christ (Ephesians 2:4-5).

You're Blessed

Praise be to the God and Father of our Lord Jesus Christ, who has blessed us in the heavenly realms with every spiritual blessing in Christ (Ephesians 1:3).

You're Chosen by God

For he chose us in him before the creation of the world to be holy and blameless in his sight. In love (Ephesians 1:4).

But you are a chosen people, a royal priesthood, a holy nation, God's special possession, that you may declare the praises of him who called you out of darkness into his wonderful light (1 Peter 2:9).

You Belong to God

Consequently, you are no longer foreigners and strangers, but fellow citizens with God's people and also members of his household, built on the foundation of the apostles and prophets, with Christ Jesus himself as the chief cornerstone. In him the whole building is joined together and rises to become a holy temple in the Lord. And in him you too are being built together to become a dwelling in which God lives by his Spirit (Ephesians 2:19-22).

You Are More Than A Conqueror

If you're struggling with your identity or are hurting and really down on yourself, read Romans 8. You are a conqueror, and *nothing* can separate you from God's love!

No, in all these things we are more than conquerors through him who loved us (Romans 8:37).

You Have Access to the Father

For through him we both have access to the Father by one Spirit (Ephesians 2:18).

In him we were also chosen, having been predestined according to the plan of him who works out everything in conformity with the purpose of his will (Ephesians 1:11).

You're Included with Christ

And you also were included in Christ when you heard the message of truth, the gospel of your salvation. When you believed, you were marked in him with a seal, the promised Holy Spirit, who is a deposit guaranteeing our inheritance until the redemption of those who are God's possession—to the praise of his glory (Ephesians 1:13-14).

You're Redeemed and Forgiven

In him we have redemption through his blood, the forgiveness of sins, in accordance with the riches of God's grace that he lavished on us (Ephesians 1:7-8).

You're the Light of the World

You are the salt of the earth. But if the salt loses its saltiness, how can it be made salty again? It is no longer good for anything, except to be thrown out and trampled underfoot. You are the light of the world. A town built on a hill cannot be hidden (Matthew 5:13-14).

You're Known by God

Indeed, the very hairs of your head are all numbered. Don't be afraid; you are worth more than many sparrows (Luke 12:7).

Before I formed you in the womb I knew you, before you were born I set you apart; I appointed you as a prophet to the nations (Jeremiah 1:5).

You have searched me, Lord, and you know me. You know when I sit and when I rise; you perceive my thoughts from afar. You discern my going out and my lying down; you are familiar with all my ways. Before a word is on my tongue you, Lord, know it completely. You hem me in behind and before, and you lay your hand upon me. Such knowledge is too wonderful for me, too lofty for me to attain.

Where can I go from your Spirit? Where can I flee from your presence? If I go up to the heavens, you are there; if I make my bed in the depths, you are there. If I rise on the wings of the dawn, if I settle on the far side of the sea, even there your hand will guide me, your right hand will hold me fast. If I say, "Surely the darkness will hide me and the light become night around me," even the darkness will not be dark to you; the night will shine like the day, for darkness is as light to you.

For you created my inmost being; you knit me together in my mother's womb. I praise you because I am fearfully and wonderfully made; your works are wonderful, I know that full well. My frame was not hidden from you when I was made in the secret place, when I was woven together in the depths of the earth. Your eyes saw my unformed body; all the days ordained for me were written in your book before one of them came to be. How precious to me are your thoughts, God! How vast is the sum of them! Were I to count them, they would outnumber the grains of sand—when I awake, I am still with you (Psalm 139:1-18).

Many people live a miserable Christian life, in despair and torment, just because they don't know or believe in their identity in Christ. Knowing yourself and who you are in Christ is crucial for your deliverance. Once you are secure about your identity in Christ, no one will be able to change your mind about your identity. You will have the power and authority to defeat Satan and his demons.

Powerful Tips

❖ *In Matthew 4, the devil told Jesus; "If You are the Son of God." If! He even dared to attack the identity of Jesus Christ. He knew if he destroyed His identity first, the rest would be easy.*

❖ *In the same way, the enemy attacks your identity and labels you with lies. When you choose to believe God's truth about you instead of the devil's lies about you, you are powerful and victorious.*

❖ *Declare: "I am a child of God."*

3. Know Your Enemy

Your enemy is Satan—Lucifer, the devil—and his demons. Lucifer (meaning Light-bearer) was one of the most beautiful and powerful of God's angels, and he was kicked out of heaven when he tried to exalt himself in the place of God and sit on His throne. He was cast down from heaven because of his rebellion, which was caused by his pride (see Isa. 14:12-20; Luke 10:18; Rev. 12:7-12; Gen. 3:1-5).

After his rebellion, he was called Satan (adversary, opposer, resister), and also the devil (slanderer and accuser). He deceived many angels into following him in his rebellion, and they are demons today. He is also called "serpent," "roaring lion," "morning star," and other names that are consistent with his character as the "tempter" or "deceiver."

Satan Is Merciless and Hates You

You need to understand and believe that the devil is the number-one enemy of God and the number-one enemy of you and your family. He is vicious and merciless. The Scripture describes him as a roaring lion, prowling around looking for someone to devour (see 1 Pet. 5:8). Once I saw a lion on an animal channel waiting quietly and patiently to attack a zebra. When he found the opportune moment, he attacked the zebra from the back and devoured him viciously. The scene was so bloody that I couldn't continue watching it. But I want you to get the idea.

You are created in God's own image (see Gen. 1:27). Because Satan hates God, he hates you and me too because we are all created in God's image.

Satan Is a Liar

Jesus called the devil the father of all lies: "There is no truth in him. When he lies, he speaks his native language, for he is a liar and the father of lies" (John 8:44).

You need to understand that he is going to lie to you about everything concerning you in order to deceive you and steal your freedom, happiness, success, and everything God has planned for your life. Ultimately, he wants to steal and destroy your life by bringing suicidal thoughts to your mind and speaking lies to you about your life.

Satan Is a Supernatural Being

Satan is a supernatural being. His followers, which are impure spirits—or demons, in other words—are also supernatural beings. This is the very reason you cannot win a battle against Satan and his demons with your natural or carnal weapons.

> *The weapons we fight with are not the weapons of the world. On the contrary, they have divine power to demolish strongholds* (2 Corinthians 10:4).

In Daniel 8:25, part of the message God's angel Gabriel delivers to Daniel was that Satan will not be destroyed by human power. Many times, we engage in warfare or try to fight spiritual attacks of the devil by our own human power and get defeated and discouraged. However, if we fight our battles with God's supernatural power, we will have victory.

Satan Is an Imitator

There is only one Creator—our God, Yahweh, I AM, Yeshua Hamashia, Jesus Christ. The devil and all his armies of demons together cannot stand against our God. He can only imitate what God has created and twist and corrupt it.

Satan masquerades himself as an angel of light (see 2 Cor. 11:14). One major craftiness of the devil is his ability to imitate and disguise. This is the very reason people without discernment can be easily deceived by the moves of familiar spirits, which are demons, rather than the move of the Holy Spirit.

Satan Is a Thief

The enemy of our soul, Satan, is described in the Bible as a thief.

> *The thief comes only to steal and kill and destroy; I have come that they may have life, and have it to the full* (John 10:10).

The devil tries to steal your joy, peace, happiness, success, calling, family, finances, and every single blessing you can think of in your life. He is also a murderer and is after your life and the lives of your loved ones. He injects suicidal thoughts into people's minds over a long period of time until they are completely under his influence and are ready to end their lives. He is a destroyer. He wants to destroy you, your family, your life, your marriage, your finances, your reputation, and every single inheritance you have from God.

The Enemy Has a Voice

Many Christians believe that the moment they receive Christ as their Lord and Savior they only hear from God. Many people also think that whatever they hear in their mind is their own thought process. This is far from the truth. The devil can speak to you in your first-person voice. This may be shocking to you, but as I mentioned earlier, he is an imitator. He is trying to imitate God. He is trying to imitate your own voice to deceive you.

In the Word of God, the serpent spoke to Eve in the Garden of Eden (see Gen. 3:1-5); the devil spoke to Jesus (see Matt. 4); Jesus told Peter, "Get behind me, Satan" (Peter wasn't Satan, but he was Satan's mouthpiece); and Satan incited David to number God's army (see 1 Chron. 21:1).

On the day I was planning my suicide, there was a voice in my head telling me, "Life is not worth living." This voice sounded like my own voice. What do you think *now* about whose voice it was?

Is that voice that sounds like your own thoughts telling you lies about yourself, your life, about others, and even lies about God? Are you making an agreement with Satan by believing those lies? Some of the common lies we hear people say are:

- No good thing ever happens to me.
- If something good happens, something bad will happen right afterward.
- I am a reject.
- No one loves me.
- No one cares for me.
- I am fat.
- I am ugly.
- I am stupid.
- I am not good enough.
- I always fail.
- I am a failure.
- God left me.
- God is angry with me.
- God hates me.
- God doesn't like me.
- I have no gifts or talents.
- I am not good at anything.
- I am stuck in my circumstances.
- I am hopeless.
- There is no way out.
- No one can help me.

Do any of these sound familiar to you?

The Devil and His Demons Use People

The word for "spirit" in Hebrew is *ruwach* and in Greek is *pneuma*. Both words mean breath, wind, and breeze. This is the same for the spirit portion of the Holy Spirit. There is only one Holy Spirit, but there are many impure demonic spirits. When we say *Holy Spirit*, we are referring to God's Spirit, which is omnipotent and omnipresent. Anyone can be either full of the Holy Spirit or full of demonic spirits.

Demons are invisible, impure spirits that need bodies to operate from. In other words, they need people to enter into and perform evil from. When a person opens a door to them through sin, tragedies, trauma, evil practices, false religions and occult practices, rebellion, disobedience, horror movies, violent or sexual movies, pornography, satanic pacts, or other ungodly practices, demons start residing in that person.

Pride itself is an open door to demons. I have seen people who live extremely religious, moral, and decent lives who are full of demons just because of their pride. Lucifer was kicked out of heaven because of his pride, and he is like a magnet to those who are prideful and arrogant. People who are addicted to looking and acting perfectly (which is the Pharisee spirit) and who judge others in their hearts are easy targets for the demonic.

The Enemy Is a Bully and an Intimidator

The man of God, Elijah, was bullied by Queen Jezebel, and he was afraid. Don't judge the man! We are nothing but flesh and blood. Everybody has a limit. I don't care how spiritual you are, you have a limit. But the moment you stop listening to and obeying the voice of God due to fear, tiredness, or whatever, you are in a dangerous place.

The enemy is the tempter (see Matt. 4), accuser (see Rev. 12:10-11), and murderer (John 8:44), and he has many more wicked qualities in his personality. However, like all bullies he must crumble before a greater power, and we have that very power on our side—the blood of Jesus Christ! No matter how powerful the devil and his demons are, if you belong to Jesus you can exercise authority over him and kick him out! We will go more into this in the next chapters.

Powerful Tips

- ✠ *Your tongue is your sword.*
- ✠ *Your praise is your weapon—your machine gun!*
- ✠ *Your mouth is your ammunition.*
- ✠ *Your thanksgiving is a gigantic magnet to miracles and breakthroughs.*
- ✠ *Open your mouth! Declare and win!*
- ✠ *Maybe until now you used your weapon against yourself and others. From now on, open your mouth to destroy the work of the enemy in your life and in the lives of your loved ones. Take your life back with your declarations.*

Chapter 8

SEVEN STEPS TO PREPARE FOR YOUR SELF-DELIVERANCE

Knowing the three basic things covered in the last chapter is the most vital preparation for any deliverance, including self-deliverance. But beyond that, there are several steps you can take to prepare yourself, if an experienced deliverance minister is not available and you are venturing into this for yourself. These seven steps will guide you, give you a structure to follow, and help you proceed with confidence into your freedom. They are:

1. Proclaim God's Word out loud.
2. Praise and worship God.
3. Bind and loose.
4. Use the blood of Jesus in prayer.
5. Cast out your fear.
6. Remove any hindering spirits or thoughts.
7. Forgive.

1. Proclaim God's Word Out Loud

Why out loud? Because the devil is called the prince of the air (see Eph. 2:2)! Therefore, we must be vocal with our declarations, praises, and warfare prayers to defeat the enemy. This is the very reason the Word of God is called the Sword of the Spirit (see Eph. 6:17). If you don't take your sword out of its sheath, how can you use it? Taking your Bible in your hands and declaring out loud the Word of God is how you use your sword, which is your divine weapon against Satan and his armies.

David didn't go before Goliath in silence. He won his battle before he threw the stone by the declaration that came out loud from his mouth.

> *David said to the Philistine, "You come against me with sword and spear and javelin, but I come against you in the name of the Lord Almighty, the God of the armies of Israel, whom you have defied. This day the Lord will deliver you into my hands, and I'll strike you down and cut off your head. This very day I will give the carcasses of the Philistine army to the birds and the wild animals, and the whole world will know that there is a God in Israel. All those gathered here will know that it is not by sword or spear that the Lord saves; for the battle is the Lord's, and he will give all of you into our hands"* (1 Samuel 17:45-47).

Look at the young shepherd boy David's faith. Look at his declaration. Look at the glorification and exaltation of His God, Yahweh. All of this he declared aloud.

When Saul was tormented by an evil spirit, David played anointed worship music and the evil spirit left Saul (see 1 Sam. 16:14-23).

Gideon won a battle with only 300 men against a vast army just by shouting, "For the Lord and for Gideon" (Judg. 7:18,20).

The walls of Jericho collapsed when the Israelites shouted and blew trumpets and marched around the city for seven days (see Josh. 6:1-20).

Jehoshaphat and his army won a battle against a vast army by singing and praising the Lord and saying, "Give thanks to the Lord, for his love endures forever" (2 Chron. 20:21).

Faith comes through hearing the Word of God (see Rom. 10:17).

You need faith to do self-deliverance. You must believe that God is on your side and that you will be free. You need a faith boost. If you don't read the Word out loud, how can you hear the Word?

Proclaim the following personalized deliverance Scriptures out loud:

> *No weapon formed against me shall prosper, and every tongue which rises against me in judgment I shall condemn. This is the heritage of the servants of the Lord, and my righteousness is from the Lord* (Isaiah 54:17).

> *When the enemy comes in like a flood, the Spirit of the Lord will raise up a standard against him* (Isaiah 59:19).

> *I overcome the devil by the blood of the Lamb and by the word of my testimony, that I am a child of God* (Revelation 12:11).

> *In righteousness I shall be established; I shall be far from oppression, for I shall not fear; and from terror, for it shall not come near me* (Isaiah 54:14).

> *For the weapons of my warfare are not carnal, but mighty in God for pulling down strongholds* (2 Corinthians 10:4).

> *In addition to all this, I take up the shield of faith, with which I can extinguish all the flaming arrows of the evil one. I take*

the helmet of salvation and the sword of the Spirit, which is the word of God (Ephesians 6:16-17).

Christ has redeemed me from the curse of the law, having become a curse for me, for it is written: "Cursed is everyone who is hung on a tree" (Galatians 3:13).

I am from God and have overcome them, because the One who is in me is greater than the one who is in the world (1 John 4:4).

I stand therefore, having fastened on the belt of truth, and having put on the breastplate of righteousness, and, as shoes for my feet, having put on the readiness given by the gospel of peace (Ephesians 6:14-17).

He has delivered me from the power of darkness, and has translated me into the kingdom of His dear Son (Colossians 1:13).

Jesus has given me authority to trample on snakes and scorpions and to overcome all the power of the enemy; nothing will harm me (Luke 10:19).

For God has not given me a spirit of fear, but of power and of love and of a sound mind (2 Timothy 1:7).

Praise be to the God and Father of my Lord Jesus Christ, who has blessed me in the heavenly realms with every spiritual blessing in Christ (Ephesians 1:3).

But He was pierced for my transgressions, He was crushed for my iniquities; the punishment that brought me peace was on Him, and by His wounds I am healed (Isaiah 53:5).

You are my Shepherd, Lord God. I lack nothing. You take me to green pastures. You lead me to quiet waters. You lead me in the paths of righteousness for Your Name's sake. You restore my soul. Even though I walk through the valley of the shadow of death, I will fear no evil, for You are with me. You prepare a table before me in the presence of my enemies; You anoint my head with oil; my cup overflows. Surely goodness and mercy shall follow me all the days of my life, and I shall dwell in the house of the Lord forever (Psalm 23).

I heal the sick, raise the dead, cleanse those who have leprosy, drive out demons. Freely I have received; freely I give (Matthew 10:8).

I am more than a conqueror through Jesus who loves me (Romans 8:37).

All things work together for good for those who love God (Romans 8:28).

If God is for me, who can be against me? (Romans 8:31)

I don't fear the enemy, for the Lord my God will fight for me (Deuteronomy 3:22).

God disarmed the principalities and powers and made a bold display and public example of them, in triumphing over them by the cross (Colossians 2:15).

Without a doubt my Lord Jesus will certainly deliver and draw me to Himself from every assault of evil. He will preserve and bring me safe unto His heavenly kingdom. To Him be the glory forever and ever. Amen (2 Timothy 4:18).

For if, by the trespass of the one man, death reigned through that one man, how much more will I, who have received God's abundant provision of grace and the gift of righteousness, reign in life through the one man, Jesus Christ! (Romans 5:17)

The thief comes only to steal and kill and destroy. Jesus came that I may have life and have it abundantly (John 10:10).

But if I walk in the light, as He is in the light, I have fellowship with others, and the blood of Jesus, His Son, purifies me from all sin (1 John 1:7).

God made Him who had no sin to be sin for me, so that in Him I might become the righteousness of God (2 Corinthians 5:21).

Whoever dwells in the shelter of the Most High will rest in the shadow of the Almighty (Psalm 91:1).

No harm will overtake me, no disaster will come near my tent (Psalm 91:10).

I am in complete agreement with Paul's prayer that:

Out of His glorious riches He may strengthen me with power through His Spirit in my inner being so that Christ may dwell in my heart through faith. I, being rooted and established in love, have the power, together with all the Lord's holy people, to grasp how wide and long and high and deep is the love of Christ, and to know this love that surpasses knowledge—that I may be filled to the measure of all the fullness of God (Ephesians 3:16-19).

2. Praise and Worship God

Praise brings victory. When you exalt God, the devil shrinks and shrinks and becomes nothing. The best way to start self-deliverance is through praise and worship.

> *The Lord is my light and my salvation—whom shall I fear? The Lord is the stronghold of my life—of whom shall I be afraid?* (Psalm 27:1)

Declare these praises aloud to Him:

- Lord Jesus, You are my High Priest (Hebrews 4:14-16)
- You are my Prince of Peace (Isaiah 9:6)
- You are my Rock (Psalm 18:2)
- You are my Deliverer (Psalm 18:2)
- You are my Stronghold and Deliverer (Psalm 144:2)
- You are the Lord (Exodus 6:2-3)
- You are Lord of Earth (Joshua 3:13)
- You are Lord Creator (Isaiah 40:28)
- You are Lord the Sword (Deuteronomy 33:29)
- You are Lord my God (Psalm 18:2)
- You are Lord Most High (Psalm 38:2)
- You are Mighty in Battle (Psalm 24:8)
- You are Lord my Defense (Psalm 89:18)
- You are Lord My Redeemer (Isaiah 49:26; 60:16)
- You are Lord King (Psalm 98:6)
- You are Lord my Judge (Judges 11:27)
- You are Lord King Forever (Psalm 10:16)

- You are Lord Saves (Psalm 20:9)
- You are my Provider (Genesis 22:14; 1 John 4:9; Philippians 4:19)
- You are Lord my Glory (Psalm 3:3)
- You are Lord Jealous (Exodus 34:14)
- You are the Horn of Salvation (Psalm 18:2)
- You are Sanctifier (Exodus 31:13; 1 Corinthians 1:30)
- You are Lord my Refuge (Psalm 91:9)
- You are Lord my Shield (Deuteronomy 33:29)
- You are Lord my Fortress (Jeremiah 16:19; Psalm 18:2)
- You are Lord my Deliverer (Psalm 18:2)
- You are Lord my High Tower (Psalm 18:2)
- You are Lord who Smites (Ezekiel 7:9)
- You are my Banner (1 Chronicles 29:11-13)
- You are my Shepherd (Psalm 23)
- You are my Healer (Isaiah 53:4-5)
- You are Lord of Hosts (1 Samuel 1:3)
- You are Lord my Rock (Psalm 18:2)
- You are Peace (Isaiah 9:6; Romans 8:31-35)
- You are Present (Hebrews 13:5)
- You are Righteousness (1 Corinthians 1:30)
- You are Lord my Strength (Psalm 19:14; 27:1; 28:7)
- You are Lord my Savior (Isaiah 49:26)
- You are *the Lord Is With Me* (Judges 6:12)
- You are the Lord, Strong and Mighty (Psalm 24:8)
- You are the Lord my Light (Psalm 27:1)

- You are the Lord my Strength in Trouble (Isaiah 49:26)

3. Bind and Loose

Whatever you bind on earth will be bound in heaven, and whatever you loose on earth will be loosed in heaven (Matthew 16:19).

Binding and loosing is a powerful weapon to disarm the enemy and render him useless. Unfortunately, many Christians don't make use of this incredibly powerful tool. When I found out how effective and powerful this divine weapon was, I started applying it and putting it to use in many situations.

For example, from time to time I had to be in an environment where there was an incredible amount of strife, wickedness, and hypocrisy. I had to be subject to a person who confessed to be a Christian, but somehow, long before I knew him, he had lost his connection with the Head—that is, with Christ. He was working and functioning like a robot and had no sense or convictions. He had a faultfinding and sarcastic personality. He partnered with his helper to slander and persecute me. Even though he was in charge, he would only hear his helper's comments and accusations. This is an Ahab personality. And you can guess what the operating spirit in the other person was! He was getting the nurturing and affection he needed from his helper. This bound the soul-tie between them, and it was very strong—and demonic.

They both operated under the two principalities of the Ahab-and-Jezebel combination. These two always go hand in hand together. Where there is an Ahab, there is a Jezebel. Where there is a Jezebel, there is always an Ahab. Also, the spirit behind Ahab carries a deaf and dumb spirit.

(This is spiritual deafness and dumbness.) The person can be super intelligent with regard to IQ but is not spiritually discerning. You speak to them and get nowhere. Oftentimes they don't even answer or comment. They look disengaged and numb. You may explain things in great detail yet never get heard. This is because they are spiritually deaf, which creates something of a numbness. They have little or no convictions of the Holy Spirit. Outwardly, they may be living a self-righteous Christian life, as was the case in this man's example, but they are operating on automatic pilot, having no sense or personal relationship.

Many women in the church have husbands like this and are in deep depression, as their voices are not being heard. They are alone and wondering what is causing their misery. How did love and affection leave their marriage? And because they are the one suffering with depression, they assume they are the problem. If they could just know and realize that the enemy first disarmed and pacified their husbands, then victimized them afterward to disable their support system. Many times, I have wished their husbands had come for deliverance instead of them.

In the case of the previous example, I started binding and loosing the Jezebel and Ahab principalities in that situation, and the result was amazing. Once God revealed to me the principalities that were ruling over them, I started putting into practice the simple divine tool that Jesus gave me. I started binding the spirits of Jezebel and Ahab, and loosing God's peace, protection, love, and joy. The power of darkness backed off. The result was the proof that the principalities were an exact demonic match. If you are going through something like this, you need to fight against the principality of darkness, not the people.

Over the years, I found out how powerful binding and loosing is. Jesus taught us how to bind and loose in two Scriptures in the Book of Matthew.

Whatever you bind on earth will be bound in heaven, and whatever you loose on earth will be loosed in heaven (Matthew 16:19).

Truly I tell you, whatever you bind on earth will be bound in heaven, and whatever you loose on earth will be loosed in heaven (Matthew 18:18).

How do we bind and loose?

- Bind the principality of darkness or the demonic! Loose what is of God from heaven.

- You can also bind the demons of others to prevent their influence and harm to you. Exercise your authority in Christ!

Declarations for Binding and Loosing

Lord Jesus, according to Your Word and promise, I bind any violent display of the enemy or any plans and assignments against me and my family, and I loose freedom and peace in Your Name, Jesus, I pray. Amen.

I bind the spirit of anger, frustration, and strife and loose peace, patience, and joy. I rebuke the enemy and declare the power of the blood of Jesus over me and my family right now in Jesus' Name. Amen.

I bind the spirit of negative thinking and mind torment, and I loose peace and joy in Jesus' Name. I am covered by the blood of Jesus. Amen.

I bind and cast out fear and anxiety right now and I loose joy and calmness in Jesus' Name. I am under the blood covering and protection of Jesus Christ. Amen.

I bind the demons of gossip and slander in this place right now and loose unity and love in Jesus' Name. Amen.

Binding Prayer Before Self-Deliverance

Dear Lord Jesus,

According to Your Word, I bind the interference of the enemy and any demonic forces from my deliverance. I bind the demons of lies, deception, confusion, doublemindedness, and any violent attack during and after my deliverance, in Jesus' Name. I release Your truth, Spirit of Truth; I release Your freedom; I loose Your deliverance and redemption in the Name of Jesus Christ. Amen. I cover myself and this time with the powerful blood of Jesus. Amen.

I have seen a video where a robber was entering a store to rob the place. He pulled his gun and told the lady behind the counter to give him all the money in the register. She boldly told him, "I bind you, Satan, in the Name of Jesus. Leave my store right now, in Jesus' Name." The thief immediately left the store. (I am not telling you to do the same. You have your own responsibility in your life to protect yourself and others and to use whatever weapon you think you need in order to do that.)

My husband and I used to engage easily in arguments that resulted in big fights. When I made up my mind to defeat the devil in my marriage by fighting differently than before, I started binding the spirits of strife, anger, division, and quarrels and began loosing love, joy, and peace into my marriage and started seeing miraculous outcomes. But I had to first make up my mind that I was not ever going to answer or react to my husband the way I used to, but only in the powerful way of Jesus, who taught me this. I am a living example of this truth today.

I heard a testimony of a Christian woman whose husband was regularly beating her up. She started binding the demons behind her husband's evil act. She said when her husband was walking toward her to hit her, she would start binding, and the man would turn back and leave the room. (Again, your situation may be different. I strongly suggest that you seek the truth and the guidance of God in your situation. But I cannot emphasize more the power of binding and loosing.)

When you are binding and loosing, you don't have to yell or shout. You can bind and loose under your breath with a whisper. But still do it vocally, because the prince of the air has to hear it to be stopped.

I also release confusion, blindness, and torment over the enemy, so he cannot be in my presence without being tormented. In Mark 5, demons asked Jesus if he was going to torment them, proving that He could have done so and they knew it. *We have an authority in Christ that we must start using.*

4. Use the Blood of Jesus in Prayer

They [Christians] *triumphed over him by the blood of the Lamb and by the word of their testimony* (Revelation 12:11).

The blood of Jesus has tremendous power. Just as with binding and loosing, many Christians don't use the power of the blood. Every day I cover myself, my family, my ministry team, board, friends, and even followers with the blood of Jesus.

There were many times when demonic manifestations took place and people became monstrous to the point of extreme violence because of the strong demonic powers in them. But because of the power of the blood of Jesus over me, never could they harm me. Even though there were times it became both a physical and a spiritual battle, they couldn't hurt me. There were times demons from other people spoke to me and told me they could do this and that to me. I said, "I am under the blood protection and covering of Jesus Christ and I am a child of the living God. You cannot touch me." They backed off as soon as I declared my position in Christ.

5. Cast Out Your Fear

God has not given us a spirit [demon, because it is written with a small "s"] *of fear, but of power and of love and of a sound mind* (2 Timothy 1:7 NKJV).

There is no fear in love. But perfect love drives out fear (1 John 4:18).

What do you cast out? You cast out demons.

Receiving and trusting God's perfect and unconditional love is an automatic result of freedom from fear. If you know someone loves you perfectly, you know they will protect you and they have your best interests at heart.

Coming from Islam and worshiping a false Muslim god for almost two decades, I had a hard time accepting God's love. I was not free from fear, even though I had become a Christian, because I still believed that God was out to get me. Somehow I was believing I had to be punished for everything I had done in my past. One day, God tenderly spoke to me that I didn't know Him well enough and that I was rejecting His love. He told me that I was believing in the lies and deceptions of the devil. I was nullifying the power of the cross. I immediately repented from believing lies about God and received His love and was set free from fear.

One of the biggest weapons the devil uses against us is fear. Fear is paralyzing. Fear is tormenting. There is no peace where there is fear. There is no joy where there is fear. Fear can get you stuck, keep you bound in the same place, and waste your years.

The opposite of fear is faith. Faith comes through hearing the Word of God. Therefore, you need to exercise the declaration of the Scriptures and praise God out loud, as I taught you earlier.

Many people are afraid of self-deliverance or deliverance performed by a minister because of the possibility that the demons could manifest or shriek, and they would be embarrassed or get hurt. They think, "What if something goes out of control?"

When I shared my self-deliverance guide on social media, a lot of people wrote to me that the steps I was teaching were working, but because fear entered their hearts during their deliverance, they didn't continue and couldn't get set free.

I want to help you get rid of the fear of self-deliverance. You need to understand and believe the following:

- God loves you and wants to set you free. Your deliverance is God's will.

- Jesus died on the cross for your freedom (see Gal. 5:1).

- If you want freedom, you will have freedom:

    Which of you, if your son asks for bread, will give him a stone? Or if he asks for a fish, will give him a snake? If you, then, though you are evil, know how to give good gifts to your children, how much more will your Father in heaven give good gifts to those who ask him! (Matthew 7:9-11)

As I mentioned before, you can bind the enemy from any violent manifestation and command it or them to leave quietly.

I bind you, devil, in the Name of Jesus, and you will leave peacefully and quietly with your demons, in Jesus' Name. I am under the blood covering of Jesus; you cannot touch me. Amen.

God is merciful. Do you believe that you will be doing self-deliverance to kick the enemy out of your life and God will hand you over to Satan or his demons? *No!* He is on your side because the devil is His enemy. But you must trust Him fully.

First you need to know there are three types of fear:

Fear of Evil/Demons

Every fear that is not fear of God is demonic. If you're afraid of demons, this too is from demons. Demonic fears make up a long list:

- Fear of accidents
- Fear of poverty
- Fear of dying alone
- Fear of sickness
- Fear of abandonment
- Fear of rejection
- Fear of failure
- Fear of people
- Fear of terror
- Fear of death

- Fear of dark
- Fear of close spaces
- Fear of losing a job

These are all demonic fears that come from the devil and from not trusting God.

Fear That Comes from Not Being Right with God

This type of fear is very close to the previous one. Not being right with God opens a door to the enemy.

I know a young girl who was extremely fearful. She was living a double life (she was only attracted to married men, as she confessed, and tried to wreck their marriages). She ruined her best friend's marriage, and many married and older men in the ministry were seduced by her. She was living in constant fear of being exposed. Later, when it was exposed, she confessed that she had always been fearful that one day God would reveal all she had been doing in secret. Even the male leadership were under her demonic spell and were secretly in love with her. These were all married men. But the curses and misery that came upon them were undeniable. Their lives, marriages, and children have suffered greatly. The wicked live in fear.

> *The wicked flee though no one pursues, but the righteous are bold as a lion* (Proverbs 28:1).

If you fear people, you need to ask yourself if there is anything in you that is not right with God. Or, if you fear and despise authority, the root cause is a rebellious heart.

Once someone prophesied over me that the devil was afraid of me. Immediately, the Holy Spirit bore witness in my heart. Later, many times demons spoke through people during their deliverance, saying they were afraid of me. That in itself was evidence of the demonic possession or oppression of an individual. You need to understand that demons can also oppress an individual with that kind of fear.

Fear of God

This is the only scriptural fear any of us should have. This fear is not like in Islam, that we should dread and be terrified of our God. But it is a healthy, reverential fear of God, knowing that if we do not live a life that pleases Him, we will face consequences that would not be pleasant.

6. Remove Hindering Spirits or Thoughts

In Mark 9, Jesus addressed a hindrance before the deliverance.

> So they brought him. When the spirit saw Jesus, it immediately threw the boy into a convulsion. He fell to the ground and rolled around, foaming at the mouth.
>
> Jesus asked the boy's father, "How long has he been like this?"
>
> "From childhood," he answered. "It has often thrown him into fire or water to kill him. But if you can do anything, take pity on us and help us."
>
> "'If you can'?" said Jesus. "Everything is possible for one who believes."
>
> Immediately the boy's father exclaimed, "I do believe; help me overcome my unbelief!"

When Jesus saw that a crowd was running to the scene, he rebuked the impure spirit. "You deaf and mute spirit," he said, "I command you, come out of him and never enter him again."

The spirit shrieked, convulsed him violently and came out. The boy looked so much like a corpse that many said, "He's dead." But Jesus took him by the hand and lifted him to his feet, and he stood up.

After Jesus had gone indoors, his disciples asked him privately, "Why couldn't we drive it out?"

He replied, "This kind can come out only by prayer" (Mark 9:20-29).

Hindering spirits will try to stop your deliverance! These demons may not be the most immediately obvious ones. Many times, people are aware of a sin issue they are struggling with—or you may be able to clearly see that a certain sin is operating in their lives—but before you can address the demons behind that sin, there are often some subtler demons "guarding the door." They will hinder any attempt at deliverance unless they are bound and cast out first, as in the following examples.

Lies and Deception

The spirit of lies and deception is one of the major hindrances to deliverance and is usually the first demon to be cast out.

I was ministering deliverance to a lady who had many demons. After spending some time getting nowhere, I stopped and started praying, which is what I usually do if the deliverance is taking a long time. I said, "Holy Spirit, Spirit of Truth, please reveal to me what is hindering her deliverance. In Jesus' Name I ask. Amen." As soon as I prayed, it was revealed that she was a victim of a Satanic ceremony at age three and had been forced to drink human blood. But this was not what was hindering her deliverance.

She believed that because she was part of such a Satanic ritual, there was no hope for her. That was the lie and deception, because there is always hope in Christ. No matter how radical the Satanic involvement or encounter or how terrible the past sins that were committed, there is always hope. What the enemy wants to do is tell you there is no hope for you. If you believe you cannot be delivered, you cannot be delivered.

Through many experiences, I have learned that when performing deliverance on a homosexual person, the first demon that needs to be cast out is not homosexuality. It is the demon of lies and deception. This is because many believe they are born that way and that God created them that way. You need to remove the demon of lies and deception to expel the demons of perversion.

Disbelief

No one can exercise deliverance against a person's will. I had a woman come to the altar at one of my meetings and order me: "Do your thing. I guess I need deliverance." I simply walked away. Her disbelief was obvious in her grudging attitude. Again, if you believe you cannot be delivered, you cannot be delivered.

Doubt

Another woman came to the altar and asked for a prayer for deliverance. I asked if she believed she could be delivered. She said, "Maybe." She had no faith that Jesus could deliver her, but she did have the will to seek deliverance. First, we prayed for faith and read a few Scriptures. Then I asked if she believed she could get delivered. This time, she had no hesitation that she could, and she was set free in moments.

Denial

Denial of the need for deliverance is also a hindrance. There have been some people who came asking for prayer who were very superficial and casual in their approach. They were not aware of the seriousness of their captivity.

One young girl who had had many abortions was unable to confess them as murder. She couldn't get delivered until she completely broke down under the conviction of the Holy Spirit and confessed and repented from murder. I am not being judgmental here. Before accepting the Lord Jesus as my Lord and Savior, I had two abortions. I carried guilt and shame even during my Christian walk until one day I had to call it as it is, *murder*, and repent. I immediately received forgiveness and was set free from guilt and shame.

Another lady who was addicted to masturbation could not confess her sin of masturbation. She could not accept it as a sin. I told her there was nothing I could do for her freedom. Without repentance, there is just no way that demon is going to leave.

If you want to stay dignified and your pride means more to you than your freedom, you can't be delivered. Humbling yourself before the Lord brings so much redemption, while holding on to your pride empowers Satan and his demons.

Doublemindedness

Doublemindedness is another serious hindrance that can prevent a person's freedom.

You must settle these questions between you and the Lord:

- Can Jesus deliver me?
- Is it God's will for me to be free?
- Does God want me to be free?
- Can I be truly set free after all my sins, abuse, demonic encounters, and even if I sold my soul to the devil? Is deliverance possible for me?
- Is this that easy?
- Is this happening or are we just going along with this ritual?
- Is my deliverance taking place?
- Is this deliverance for me?
- What if the enemy hurts me?
- What if the devil throws me to the floor and foam comes from my mouth and everyone will see me like that?
- Will it be embarrassing that I will look like a mess?
- What if I don't have enough faith for this deliverance?
- I have so many sins in my life, I am not worthy of this. Can this backfire on me?

You need to know that Jesus died on the cross to settle all the above questions and doubts for you! It is finished! Jesus made it easy. He made a way!

Prayer Against Hindering Spirits

Dear Lord Jesus,

I put myself under Your authority. I declare that You are my Lord and Savior and You have given me authority to expel demons. You died on the cross to set me free from my sins, curses, chains, and sicknesses. Based on the authority You have given me, I bind all hindering spirits and command doubt, disbelief, lies, and deceptions to leave me in Jesus' Name. I bind the voice of the enemy and his lies in Jesus Christ's Name. I invite the Holy Spirit, Spirit of Truth, and His freeing power into my life in Jesus' Name. Amen!

7. Forgive

Forgiveness is a crucial part of your deliverance. If you are holding any grudges or have bitterness and resentment in your heart toward anyone, you cannot be free. Unforgiveness opens a door to the demonic. I suggest you go before the Lord and ask the Holy Spirit to reveal to you if there is anyone in your life or in your past who has hurt you and whom you haven't forgiven. If God shows you that, you can then ask Him to give you the ability to forgive.

Powerful Tips

- *Some deliverance is a process and takes place with counseling and the agape love of God.*
- *Sometimes we almost try to convince ourselves, others, and even God with long and religious prayers. Faith is activated*

when we command the devil to flee, sickness to leave, or peace and joy to come in.

✤ *Jesus said, "Pick up your mat and walk." He didn't pray for the sick but commanded sickness to leave. Now He is telling us, "Follow Me."*

✤ *Be free in Jesus' Name!*

✤ *Be filled with joy in Jesus' Name!*

✤ *Be healed in Jesus' Name!*

✤ *Be delivered in Jesus' Name!*

✤ *Start activating your faith by your words and exercising authority over your situation.*

Chapter 9

STEP BY STEP
SELF-DELIVERANCE

They brought a lady to me with a severe skin disease, with boils and red marks all over her body. I had a hard time even looking at her skin. I had never seen anything of that level before. She was covered with terrible, huge marks all over her. She was in such despair. She said that doctors told her this was incurable. When the doctors can't diagnose or say something is incurable, I personally believe it is demonic.

I started praying over her. Her eyes started rolling back and she started shaking, as many do in demonic possession. But there was not an instant healing and deliverance. Again, I sought help from the Holy Spirit: "Holy Spirit, Spirit of Truth, please reveal to me the root of this and set this woman free." Immediately our faithful Lord responded, "Her skin reflects the condition of her heart. What is in her heart has manifested on her skin. Send her home to seek after Me. You cannot do this. She has to seek me and repent from many things that I will reveal to her. Then she will be healed completely."

I told her exactly what the Holy Spirit told me. She didn't like it. People usually want instant, quick results, right then and there. They don't like to receive an assignment in place of the relief they are looking for. Deliverance has very little to do with the minister. The minister is only the facilitator. The two major persons in any deliverance are Jesus and the person who wants to be delivered.

Later on, this lady called my live TV program and testified that she went home and found a quiet place. She had never heard from the Holy Spirit before. She prayed in Jesus' Name, asking the Holy Spirit to reveal everything in her heart and to receive her freedom. As the Holy Spirit started revealing things to her one by one, she began repenting of rage, bitterness, unforgiveness, and other ugliness that was in her heart. She wept and wept before the Lord, and as she repented and asked forgiveness, her skin began clearing up right in front of her very eyes. She was completely healed when she called me and testified on TV.

Ask and Seek the Holy Spirit to Reveal

To *seek* means "desperately beg and inquire." The parable of the persistent widow is a good example from Scripture of someone who was *seeking* her deliverance (see Luke 18:1). She was desperate enough to push through a crowd and risk all kinds of ridicule and even punishment. And she was healed! Jesus also told us to seek first His kingdom (see Matt. 6:33). And our loving Father has said, "You will seek me and find me when you seek me with all your heart" (Jer. 29:13).

Ask the Holy Spirit

Dear Lord Jesus,

Please search me and show me if there is any impurity or demonic indwelling that needs to be removed from me. I trust You, Lord Jesus, to please reveal it to me. Holy Spirit, Spirit of Truth, please expose any demonic influences trespassing or residing in me that are blocking God's freedom and blessings in my life. I want to walk in Your freedom and joy. In Your Name I pray, amen.

Usually the very first thing the Holy Spirit brings to your mind right after the prayer is what He would have you look at. You don't have to push hard or overthink. You will only get more confused. Once He reveals His truth to you and shows you where the door was opened, you can go to the next step to confess it.

Confess Your Sins

Confess your sins and take responsibility for opening doors to the enemy. After the Holy Spirit reveals what needs to be removed from your life, identify them one by one and confess them. This part is very important for your freedom. List things and actions in your life that opened doors to the demonic forces, such as occult practices, false religions, divination, sorcery, fortune telling, rape, abuse, abandonment, suicide in the family, trauma, rejection, bitterness, anger, self-hatred, etc. Start confessing them one by one and be very honest about them. You are not confessing anything that God doesn't already know. For example, if you are struggling with food addiction or overeating, call it by its name—gluttony.

Confession is a very big part of your deliverance. Denial of your condition will only hinder your freedom from demonic influences. Remember it takes humility to confess our sins and pride to hide or deny them.

Sample Confession (Fear)

Dear Lord Jesus,

I confess that I have a spirit of fear. This spirit entered into me when I was a child and this event occurred:

_____

_____

_____

_____

I didn't allow you to work in me and set me free. I opened the door wider to the enemy by watching horror movies to feed the fear in me. I confess that I didn't trust You completely.

Whoever conceals their sins does not prosper, but the one who confesses and renounces them finds mercy (Proverbs 28:13).

Therefore confess your sins to each other and pray for each other so that you may be healed [cured, made whole] *(James 5:16).*

Repent and Renounce

If they have a change of heart in the land where they are held captive, and repent and plead with you in the land of their captivity and say, "We have sinned, we have done wrong and acted wickedly"; and if they turn back to you with all their heart and soul in the land of their captivity where they were taken, and pray toward the land you gave their ancestors, toward the city you have chosen and toward the temple I have built for your Name; then from heaven, your dwelling place, hear their prayer and their pleas, and uphold their cause. And forgive your people, who have sinned against you (2 Chronicles 6:37-39).

So repent [change your inner self—your old way of thinking, regret past sins] and return [to God—seek His purpose for your life], so that your sins may be wiped away [blotted out, completely erased], so that times of refreshing may come from the presence of the Lord [restoring you like a cool wind on a hot day] (Acts 3:19 AMP).

Repentance is *key* to deliverance. It takes humility to repent. People who blame others for their sins and failures are not sincere in their repentance and cannot expect a powerful result. You need to take responsibility for your mistakes, open doors, ungodly habits, addictions, or lifestyle. Denial and blame games will only keep you longer as a slave to the devil.

After we identify and confess how we opened our doors to demonic influences, we need to take responsibility, repent, and renounce all of our wrongdoings, falsehoods, evil practices, and basically anything and everything we can remember that opened our doors to demonic forces.

We cannot continue to live the way we live and blame the devil for our dysfunctional lives, addictions, and bad behaviors. We need to humble ourselves and ask forgiveness for our sins that opened the doors to the enemy. In this process, list everything the Holy Spirit brings to your mind, then repent and renounce.

Prayer of Repentance

Dear Lord Jesus,

I humbly come before You acknowledging You as the ultimate authority in my life. You are my High Priest. You are my Savior and Deliverer. You died on the cross and shed Your blood for me to be free from the penalty of my sins, bondages, and sicknesses. Today, I repent from all my sins, especially the ones that opened the doors to the enemy, such as:

_____

_____

_____

_____

(List all tragic events—such as abuse, abandonment, or rejection—that took place in your life, as well as sins or evil practices such as occult, false religions, idolatry, witchcraft/sorcery, divination, spiritualism, and similar practices.)

Please forgive me, Lord Jesus, for all these sins I have committed. I renounce them.

_____

_____

_____

_____

(Renounce your sins one by one, including any occult practices, witch-craft, involvement with sorcery, horoscopes, fortune telling, psychic readings, and false religions.)

> *I break all ungodly soul-ties! And I forgive all those who hurt me, abused me, and betrayed me (list their names):*

_____

_____

_____

_____

> *I bless them. Wash me clean with Your precious blood, dear Jesus, from **all** impurity and demonic residency or influence. I receive Your freedom. Amen.*

Cast Out

> *And these signs will accompany those who believe: In my name they will drive out demons; they will speak in new tongues* (Mark 16:17).

You are now ready to kick the enemy out of your life. This is an eviction *you* will command. You must be serious and bold when you do this. Now, command the enemy (impure, evil spirits) to leave you in Jesus' Name. Stand on your authority in Christ to expel them. In this process, name them one by one and command them to leave in the Name of Jesus Christ. You need to know the devil is a vicious creature and he may try to resist your command. Be strong in your faith and mean what you say. The enemy cannot resist when someone full of faith is kicking him out from his residence in the Name of Jesus. I have seen people in the past asking the devil politely, "Please leave," and nothing took place. But I have also seen desperate people coming against the enemy in the Name of Jesus, full of faith and standing firm. These people were gloriously delivered from the enemy.

Prayer for Casting Out

I am a child of the living God. I am under the blood of Jesus Christ. Jesus Christ is my Lord, my Savior, my Deliverer. In the Name of Jesus, I command you

_____

_____

_____

_____

(demon of lies, lust, pornography, rage, perversion, rebellion, Jezebel, Python, hostility, drugs, suicide, depression, oppression, etc.) to leave me immediately. I am a temple of the Holy Spirit. Get out in the Name of Jesus!

You need to mean business. Have no fear whatsoever. You are a child of God. He will not allow any demon to play with you or torment you unless you doubt and let fear enter in. If fear or doubt begins to enter in, you must verbally cast it out.

In the process you may be releasing/letting go of those demons through crying, yawning, excessive sweating, burping, or flatulence, all of which are simply releases from your body in different ways.

Apply the Blood of Jesus and Praise God

They triumphed over him by the blood of the Lamb and by the word of their testimony; they did not love their lives so much as to shrink from death (Revelation 12:11).

The devil hates the blood of Jesus and hates when we praise and worship God, because he wants to be worshiped. After your freedom, start covering yourself and your household with the blood of Jesus, then begin praising and worshiping God. The best way to keep the enemy out of your presence is to continuously praise and worship Jesus. Give all the glory, honor, gratitude, and recognition to Jesus for your freedom.

Dear Lord Jesus,

Thank You for delivering me from the power of the devil and his demons. I cover my deliverance with Your precious blood and I praise Your Holy Name. Thank You for setting me free from all bondages. In Your Name, Jesus, I pray. Amen.

A Prayer of Deliverance That Covers It All

Dear Lord Jesus,

I praise You and worship You. You are my Lord and Savior. You are my High Priest, Master, Healer, Deliverer, and Shepherd. You are an awesome God and I put all my trust in You. I surrender to Your will. Thank You for dying on the cross for me to be free from the penalty of my sins and for my healing and freedom.

I acknowledge and confess my sins:

_____

_____

_____

_____

I have opened the door to the enemy by doing/practicing:

_____

_____

_____

_____

I confess that I have believed in the devil's lies:

_____

_____

_____

_____

I repent and renounce all my sins:

_____

_____

_____

_____

I close all open doors to the enemy and to the ungodly and evil practices of:

_____

_____

_____

_____

I command you, devil and all your demons, to leave me in the mighty and powerful Name of Jesus Christ. I am a child of the living God and under the blood covering of Jesus Christ. I belong to the light, and darkness cannot dwell in me. You must flee right now, in Jesus' Name. You have no place in my life, nor do you have any power over me. I expel you in Jesus' Name.

(Take your time to name the demons specifically, one by one if necessary, such as: "Get out, spirit of lust; get out, spirit of insecurity; get out, spirit of pornography; get out, spirit of witchcraft," etc.)

I praise You, Lord Jesus, for setting me free from the power and influence of Satan and his demons today. I exalt Your Name, my Lord. I cover myself with Your blood. I declare that I am free from all bondages and strongholds. Thank You, Lord Jesus, for being my Redeemer. I love You and belong to You. Amen.

Powerful Tips

* ✤ *Receiving is a gift that takes faith.*
* ✤ *Receiving God's Word honors and pleases God.*
* ✤ *Jesus said, "Therefore I tell you, whatever you ask for in prayer, believe that you have received it, and it will be yours" (Mark 11:24).*
* ✤ *This is why every time you pray, receive it in the prayer in Jesus' Name, amen.*

Dear Lord Jesus,

I need Your divine wisdom. I pray that You download Your wisdom over me. I receive it in Your Name, Jesus. Amen.

_____

_____

_____

_____

Dear Lord Jesus,

I pray for Your healing touch right now and I receive my healing in Your powerful and matchless Name, amen.

_____

_____

_____

_____

Chapter 10

MAINTAINING *Your* DELIVERANCE

Meryem was my first deliverance experience that came about over the phone. Prior to praying with her, I had never done deliverance over the phone. I had been praying for a while to do a TV program on demons and deliverance, as I was receiving many letters from my viewers that they were tormented by evil spirits. I wanted to bring a biblical perspective and light to the subject, but I had no intention of doing deliverance on TV or, even later, over the phone. I knew that the subject was heavy, and I started praying and fasting for two weeks prior to the program.

During these two weeks, the enemy came against me so fiercely that I had never experienced such a demonic attack before. He tried many things to stop me from preaching and teaching about him.

Every time I was under an attack, I considered it a confirmation because I was entering into his territory and the devil was not happy. During those two weeks, it felt like hell broke lose. My husband was extremely agitated with a lot of things and began acting out. My teenage daughter was distant and treating me like an enemy. At the ministry workplace I was being slandered and facing all kinds of opposition and trials like never before, not even in the secular world. One night, our house was even shaken by a high magnitude earthquake. A lot of people are afraid of demons and the devil, but they don't consider that when you start using your authority in Christ, demons are afraid of you! The devil uses fear to stop you from exposing him and kicking him out. But you can take it because you're heading in the right direction, and you're intimidating the enemy more than he is trying to bully you. I took every attack as a confirmation that I was heading in the right direction.

After two weeks of preparation in prayer and fasting, I started a series of three live broadcasts. On the first broadcast, the phone lines were jammed. Many people called, begging for help. During the first broadcast, on air, a woman called and said on live television that she had many demons and asked for help. I told her to leave her phone number with our counselors and that I would call her after the program. I didn't even know at the time how this was going to work.

I called the number she gave and an automated voice message said it was not a valid phone number. I didn't think much about it and prayed for her during my prayer time.

The following week the same woman called again and said the same thing on the air, asking why I didn't call her. I told her I had called, but the number she left was not a working number. I asked her one more time to leave a correct number, and she agreed. Again, I called the number after my show, and again it was another invalid phone number with an automated message.

The third week she called the live show again and, in such agony and desperation, asked me why I wasn't calling her. At that very moment, I knew the demons were not allowing her to give the correct number. I asked if there was anyone near her who could give the phone number, and she said her husband was next to her. I told her that this time her husband should give the phone number to our counselors.

When I called the number, she answered. As soon as she answered there was such screaming and craziness going on that it sounded like hundreds of people next to her, ready to kill her. I asked her how many people were next to her, and she replied that only her husband was next to her. Until that moment I had never heard such violent demonic screaming. It was scarier than a horror movie soundtrack. I immediately prayed in my heart for God to strengthen me, yet I didn't know how to help her over the phone. She was calling from Europe, and I was considering finding a minister in her area who might be able to help her, but there weren't any I knew who did deliverance. In the past, whenever I needed to learn about deliverance or needed help, I couldn't find anyone to help me. While my mind was occupied with reasons why I couldn't do deliverance over the phone, the Holy Spirit revealed to me instantly that the enemy wanted to discourage me from doing such deliverance. Right away, God brought to my mind the Scripture from Matthew where the centurion told Jesus, "Just say the word." The Holy Spirit repeated several times, "Just say the Word." I immediately knew God was on my side and I had to obey His Word.

I started commanding the demons to leave one by one in the Name of Jesus Christ. The Holy Spirit was revealing their names and how they entered. As I started exercising my authority in Christ, demons started leaving her, and she began confirming that she was getting free. She started coughing heavily and also throwing up. I was taking breaks and giving her time to rest during a three-hour deliverance on the phone. She was so desperate that she would say, "It is working, please don't stop; they are leaving, please continue." After three hours she was free from 110 demons, and the following day, in half an hour, she got delivered from four more for a total of 114 demons.

Some people ask me how I knew the number of demons she was delivered from. What do you think? The same God who told me to "just say the Word" also told me the number! And He was my Guide to kick them out of her temple and set her free. After she was set free, I called her every day for three weeks and gave her a Bible study, because it is extremely important to fill your temple with the Word of God after cleaning the house. As a result of her deliverance, she also got free from many sicknesses and diseases that the demons were causing. All her fears were gone. She was able to have perfect sleep at night. She got her life back.

I can tell you a few extremely important things that played a huge role in Meryem's deliverance:

1. She was desperate.
2. She believed Jesus could deliver her.
3. She gave me full authority to do the deliverance.
4. She was humble enough to confess and renounce sins that opened the doors to the demonic.
5. She was persistent.

Can You Lose Your Deliverance?

Yes, of course you can. You *always* have free will.

There have been people who walked out from my conferences or deliverance prayer meetings free, then allowed the enemy to enter in even worse than ever before. Their latter condition was worse than their former. I stopped performing deliverance with the individuals who kept coming with the same bondage again and again after they got delivered. There is always something they are not letting go of, or are leaving the door wide open to, that allows the demons to come back.

You can close a door to the devil, but in the same way you closed that door it can be opened again. Why? *Because it is familiar to you.* You are used to that spirit. It knows how to sneak in. You need to be diligent and disciplined to keep the demon out. If you get spiritually lazy, you are inviting more trouble upon yourself. You need to fill your house (your temple) with the Word of God, prayer, praise, and worship. You cannot afford to leave your temple unoccupied. You need to be full of God and His Holy Spirit.

> *When an impure spirit comes out of a person, it goes through arid places seeking rest and does not find it. Then it says, "I will return to the house I left." When it arrives, it finds the house unoccupied, swept clean and put in order. Then it goes and takes with it seven other spirits more wicked than itself, and they go in and live there. And the final condition of that person is worse than the first. That is how it will be with this wicked generation* (Matthew 12:43-45).

Powerful Tips

* *If your emotions are ruling over you, you need both healing of your soul wounds and deliverance.*

* *When you get mad at someone, if you are speaking negativity to their future with your words, you are putting a curse on them and operating in the spirit of witchcraft and divination.*

* *Many people ask for vindication when they are actually asking for revenge. The root of it is unforgiveness and bitterness.*

After you are set free, fill the empty places with:

1. The Word of God
2. Prayer
3. Praise and worship
4. A godly lifestyle (consecrated and holy living, *not* worldly, *but godly*)

Do not believe in Satan's lies. The enemy will tell you he is back in or that he will get in. These are all his schemes and tactics.

Proclaim the Word of God!

Over the years I discovered the power of praying Scriptures. Here are some major deliverance Scriptures and prayers that I have chosen for you to declare in order to defeat the enemy:

> *"No weapon formed against you shall prosper, and every tongue which rises against you in judgment you shall condemn. This is the heritage of the servants of the Lord, and their righteousness is from Me," says the Lord* (Isaiah 54:17 NKJV).

Prayer

> *I declare that no weapon or attack coming against me will be successful. All tragedies, calamities, and harm will be halted and stopped and bear no fruit. Every judgment, false accusation, lie, curse, or evil spoken against me will fall to the ground barren and empty, in the Name of Jesus Christ, for my righteousness is in Christ Jesus and this is my heritage. Amen.*

In righteousness you will be established: Tyranny will be far from you; you will have nothing to fear. Terror will be far removed; it will not come near you (Isaiah 54:14).

Prayer

I declare that I am established in the righteousness of Jesus Christ. Because of His finished work on the cross, I will not be subject to fear any longer, and oppression is now far away from me in Jesus Christ's Name. Amen.

For the weapons of our warfare are not carnal but mighty in God for pulling down strongholds (2 Corinthians 10:4 NKJV).

Prayer

Jesus Christ, my Lord and Savior, has given me mighty weapons of warfare to fight my battles. I have the power to destroy anything that is counterfeit to the truth. When I speak the truth, all powers of hell must obey in Jesus Christ's Name, amen.

In addition to all this, take up the shield of faith, with which you can extinguish all the flaming arrows of the evil one. Take the helmet of salvation and the sword of the Spirit, which is the word of God (Ephesians 6:16-17).

Prayer

Right now, I take up the shield of faith. My faith and confidence are in You, Lord Jesus, and therefore I am shielded from any attack of the enemy. I step into each moment protected, both from the daily assaults coming toward and against me and also protected as I push forward into my destiny and my calling in Jesus Christ's Name. My mind is encompassed by the surety of my eternal salvation. This helmet of salvation soothes my mind with peace and steadies me for battle. I advance and take authority and territory today with the Sword of the Spirit. Your words, oh Lord Jesus, cut through deceit and penetrate the hearts of man. Penetrate my heart and the hearts of my family and friends, in Jesus' Name. I am well equipped in battle, and I thank You, Lord, for the victory. Amen!

Christ redeemed us from the curse of the law by becoming a curse for us—for it is written, "Cursed is everyone who is hanged on a tree" (Galatians 3:13 ESV).

Prayer

*I declare that in Jesus I am redeemed from the curse of the law. I am completely set free from all poverty, all sickness, generational curses, even spiritual and physical death in Jesus Christ's Name, amen. Jesus took all the curses that were upon me, my family, and my children onto Himself upon the cross. For that reason, I declare that I am free from **all** curses. I have eternal life in Jesus. He took the penalty of **all** my sins, past, present, and future.*

I am a child of God now, and my life is free from the curse forevermore. Amen.

You, dear children, are from God and have overcome them, because the one who is in you is greater than the one who is in the world (1 John 4:4).

Prayer

I declare that I am a child of God. I am God's beloved and overcome every enemy that is against me and my family today. There is no one greater than my Lord Jesus Christ, and because He lives inside of me I am victorious.

Stand therefore, having fastened on the belt of truth, and having put on the breastplate of righteousness, and, as shoes for your feet, having put on the readiness given by the gospel of peace (Ephesians 6:14-15 ESV).

Prayer

*I am ready to face any challenge because my foundation is rooted in the gospel of truth. Jesus is my truth and I am established in His Righteousness. His truth keeps me from stumbling and His Righteousness guards my heart as a breastplate. Knowing that He is my Lord and Savior and that He has saved me from all my sins gives me **peace** to walk out my daily life and proclaim the good news of the glorious gospel in Jesus Christ's Name, amen.*

Who hath delivered us from the power of darkness, and hath translated us into the kingdom of his dear Son (Colossians 1:13 KJV).

Prayer

*I boldly confess that I am **no longer** in darkness because Jesus Christ is my light and salvation. Jesus has delivered me and my family from the powers of the enemy. I do not stumble; I do not walk in obscurity anymore. He has placed me into the Kingdom of God, the Kingdom of His dear Son, into the light of Christ Jesus.*

I have given you authority to trample on snakes and scorpions and to overcome all the power of the enemy; nothing will harm you (Luke 10:19).

Prayer

In Jesus' Name, I rebuke any attack from the enemy in my life today. In Christ, I have been given all authority over the schemes of darkness, and nothing by any means will harm me or my loved ones in Jesus Christ's Name, amen.

For God has not given us a spirit of fear, but of power and of love and of a sound mind (2 Timothy 1:7 NKJV).

Prayer

I do not partner with a spirit of fear or bow down to it. God has given me a spirit of power, love, and a sound mind in Jesus Christ's name, amen. Therefore, I do not allow anxiety, strife, or anything contrary to the Kingdom of God to remain in my life today. I am well able and equipped in power from on high to step out and, with excellence, handle all the details of my life. I partner with the love of God, and because of His generous love I am both loving and loveable. I will walk in love toward my enemies, myself, and lavish loving praises of gratitude unto Jesus. I have a sound mind, the mind of Christ Jesus, and because of this I walk not in confusion but rather in peace and certainty. I will not wander in confusion or doubt. A sound mind, which is the mind of Jesus Christ, keeps me grounded and secure, and in the Name of Jesus I declare it, amen.

Praise be to the God and Father of our Lord Jesus Christ, who has blessed us in the heavenly realms with every spiritual blessing in Christ (Ephesians 1:3).

Prayer

I praise You, Father, for You have blessed me with every spiritual blessing in Christ Jesus. Because of You, Jesus, I am free to live the abundant life; I have eternal salvation and fellowship with Father God and Holy Spirit. I joyfully receive and acknowledge every spiritual blessing from the heavenly realm today in my life in Jesus Christ's Name, amen. This blessing spills and overflows into my life and the lives of my family so we can be a blessing to others. For You are providing for my every need out of the abundance of Your Kingdom resources in Heaven. I thank You that I lack no good thing and I receive all Your blessings today, in Jesus Christ's Name, amen.

But he was pierced for our transgressions, he was crushed for our iniquities; the punishment that brought us peace was on him, and by his wounds we are healed (Isaiah 53:5).

Prayer

I boldly confess that Jesus is my Redeemer. He took upon Himself all punishment and suffering for my past, current, and even future sins. He died for every act of my disobedience, for every lie, and for every immoral sin. By doing that, He removed my shame and guilt so I could be set free to live a life of emotional health, physical wholeness, prosperity, and eternal security. Thank You, Lord Jesus, that by Your stripes I am truly healed, saved, and set free. I declare it in Your precious Name, amen.

You prepare a table before me in the presence of my enemies; you anoint my head with oil; my cup overflows. Surely goodness and mercy shall follow me all the days of my life, and I shall dwell in the house of the Lord forever (Psalm 23:5-6 ESV).

Prayer

*I declare that no matter what my circumstances are, regardless of who or what is trying to come against me, **You**, oh Lord, prepare a place for me to dine and I partake of Your finest delicacies in*

Jesus Christ's Name. I sit down and eat at Your table, oh Lord, and You feed my spirit, soul, and body. You anoint my head with oil, as both preparation for battle and for an overflow of Your power and anointing in my life. I rejoice today in Jesus' Name because there is nowhere I can go that Your divine goodness and tender mercies cannot find me. I dwell in the house of the Lord forever. My home is in You, Lord Jesus. Amen.

Heal the sick, raise the dead, cleanse those who have leprosy, drive out demons. Freely you have received; freely give (Matthew 10:8).

Prayer

I proclaim that I am a doer of Your word in the Name of Jesus. The power of God that cleansed and set me free now lives inside of me and enables me to reach out, heal, and set others free also. You have redeemed my life and the lives of my family from destruction. I will boldly share my testimony, lay hands on the sick and hurting, and snatch those who are lost and trapped from the pit of hell, in Jesus' Name, all to the glory and in the power of our Lord Jesus Christ. Amen.

For if, by the trespass of the one man, death reigned through that one man, how much more will those who receive God's abundant provision of grace and of the gift of righteousness reign in life through the one man, Jesus Christ! (Romans 5:17).

Prayer

I thank You, Lord Jesus, for the abundant, never-ending provision of Your sweet grace. You have given unto me the beautiful gift of Your righteousness. Through Adam's sin, we all became subject to sin and were dead, yet through You, Jesus, we have been afforded life everlasting. I reign in life because of Your obedience on the cross. Thank You, Lord Jesus.

The thief comes only to steal and kill and destroy. I came that they may have life and have it abundantly (John 10:10 ESV).

Prayer

I praise You, Lord Jesus, that because You have come and conquered the enemy of my soul, You have given unto me the abundant life. The enemy can no longer steal, kill, or destroy me or my family in Jesus' Name. My portion is abundance from the throne room of heaven. You have provided unto me inexhaustible resources, both natural and supernatural. My earthly needs for food, housing, clothing, physical health, and emotional wholeness are met because of You, Lord Jesus. My mind and heart can rest knowing that I am Yours and my life is more than just here on earth but is also everlasting into eternity with You, Lord Jesus.

But if we walk in the light, as he is in the light, we have fellowship with one another, and the blood of Jesus, his Son, purifies us from all sin (1 John 1:7).

Prayer

I declare that Jesus Christ is my Lord and Savior. He is my light and salvation. His blood purifies and cleanses me of every sin. As I walk in Him, I am in fellowship and His light brings life into every relationship and circumstance in Jesus' Name, amen.

God made him who had no sin to be sin for us, so that in him we might become the righteousness of God (2 Corinthians 5:21).

Prayer

I boldly declare that I am the righteousness of God in Christ Jesus. Thank You, Lord Jesus, that because of Your finished work on the cross there is no more defeat in my life or my family's. You overcame so that my life would be full of victory and good success. You suffered the punishment of my sins for me and for my family's sake. You took it all so that I can live in Your perfect righteousness. I am in good standing with the Father, the Son, and the Holy Spirit, in Jesus' Name, amen!

The Lord will make you the head, not the tail. If you pay attention to the commands of the Lord your God that I give you this day and carefully follow them, you will always be at the top, never at the bottom (Deuteronomy 28:13).

Prayer

Thank You, Jesus, that because of Your obedience I am the head and not the tail. I will not be trampled down or left at the bottom, nor will my family. We are overcomers in Christ Jesus. I rise above every situation victorious in Jesus' Name. Amen.

You will decide on a matter, and it will be established for you, and light will shine on your ways (Job 22:28 ESV).

Prayer

I have been given all authority in the Name of Christ Jesus to decree a matter and it be done. Your light, Jesus, shines into every area of my life. As I speak Your word, changes occur, circumstances realign, the atmosphere shifts, and goodness follows in my life and in my family's lives, in the Name of Jesus, amen.

And Jesus grew in wisdom and stature, and in favor with God and man (Luke 2:52).

Prayer

I declare that as Jesus grew in wisdom and stature, I too am increasing in wisdom, in Jesus' Name. Jesus living inside of me develops me and gives me great favor with both God and man. I am not the same person I was yesterday. There is a measurable increase of knowledge and wisdom growing within me in Jesus' Name. I declare this over my children and family too. Wisdom and favor are increasing in their lives, in Jesus' mighty Name, amen.

Wealth and riches are in their houses, and their righteousness endures forever (Psalm 112:3).

Prayer

I confess that because I am in You, Lord Jesus, my righteousness endures forever. Your loving-kindness brings wealth and riches into my home for me and my family to enjoy. My household is blessed and overflowing with Your beautiful treasures from heaven above in the Name of Jesus, amen.

With long life I will satisfy him and show him my salvation (Psalm 91:16).

Prayer

Thank You, Lord. You satisfy me with long life. I shall not die prematurely or before the fulfillment of my calling here on earth. You not only provide me a plenitude of years, but also that they shall be enriched by Your salvation. The quantity of my days is extended and the quality of my life is rich and full of Your mercy and goodness in Jesus' Name. Daily, You teach me what it is to live life according to the Kingdom of Heaven. My days and the days of my family are prolonged and we are growing in the knowledge of who we are in Christ Jesus. Amen.

Whoever dwells in the shelter of the Most High will rest in the shadow of the Almighty (Psalm 91:1).

Prayer

Today, oh Lord, I choose You as the foundation of my life. This fills my heart with hope. As a child is protected in the loving arms of their parent, I run full speed ahead into Your arms. You embrace me with Your love, and I find rest in Jesus' Name. I am secure and safe in You. Amen.

No harm will overtake you, no disaster will come near your tent (Psalm 91:10).

Prayer

I boldly declare that I am completely safe. My friends, family, and loved ones are safe as well in Jesus' Name. I cast down every thought or imagined harm that exalts itself against the Word of God. I will not be overcome by fear or dread of terror because Your Word has promised that no sudden disaster will even come near me. I walk in peace and in the assurance that I am far from all harm in Jesus' Name, amen.

All your children will be taught by the Lord, and great will be their peace (Isaiah 54:13).

Prayer

My children are taught by You, Lord, and great is their peace. For the maker of heaven and earth, the Lord of lords and King of kings, teaches my children the ways of the Kingdom of God, instructs them in the night seasons, and whispers good and sweet truths over them. I relinquish the lie that it all depends on me. I thank You, Lord Jesus, that You are leading my children and guiding them into all truth. Because of this, they are established in peace in Jesus' mighty Name, amen.

I pray that out of his glorious riches he may strengthen you with power through his Spirit in your inner being, so that Christ may dwell in your hearts through faith. And I pray that you, being rooted and established in love, may have power, together with all the Lord's holy people, to grasp how wide and long and high and deep is the love of Christ, and to know this love that surpasses knowledge—that you may be filled to the measure of all the fullness of God (Ephesians 3:16-19).

Prayer

I declare that I am strengthened with power in my inner being by Your Spirit, Lord Jesus; I am rooted and grounded in Your love. I thank You that You, Jesus, dwell in my heart through faith and I am filled to the measure of all fullness in You. Your love overflows into every area of my life, increasing in measure and daily broadening my awareness of just how wide, long, high, and deep is Your amazing grace and love toward me. I thank You for Your love toward me and I fully receive it for me and my family, in Jesus' Name, amen.

Generational Curses

Another source that can interfere with your deliverance and your ability to remain delivered is a generational curse. Even the secular world acknowledges generational curses without knowing it! When you go to the doctor, you need to fill out a form where they ask about your family health history and whether your parents and grandparents have certain illnesses.

The moment you say, "My mom or dad had this sickness, now I have it," you activate the generational curse. "The apple doesn't fall far from the tree" or "Like father like son" statements empower generational curses when used in a negative way and validate the generational connection. Instead, people need to say, "My parents' or ancestors' sicknesses or curses have no power over me. I put a blood line of Jesus between me and my ancestors. I break all generational ties with the sins of my parents and their parents and grandparents in Jesus Christ's Name. Amen."

Powerful Tips

- *Reject words like, "The apple doesn't fall far from the tree," when it is used in a negative way.*
- *When dealing with generational curses, you need to look into common characteristics, behaviors, and the financial, health, and habit patterns of your ancestors.*
- *Repent from your and your forefathers' sins and cut your cords with your ancestors. Put a blood line of Jesus Christ between you and the previous generations.*

Chapter 11

OTHER METHODS *of* DELIVERANCE

1. Restoration of Trinity

Throughout my ministry, I have seen instant deliverance, followed by physical healing, just by restoration and reconciliation of an individual to one of the persons of the trinity.

I have ministered deliverance to people who had come from Muslim backgrounds, or from the Far East, or had been abandoned and rejected by their earthly fathers and who had a hard time calling on God the Father. They could call on Jesus and the Holy Spirit, but they couldn't call on the Father. There was an instant deliverance when they repented from excluding God the Father from their faith and received Him as their perfect Father.

I ministered to a young lady who couldn't embrace the Holy Spirit. She hated to hear tongues and in her past had even signed an agreement with a Bible school promising that she would never seek to speak in tongues. She manifested many demons and still couldn't embrace the Holy Spirit, even though she lived in bondage.

I am not going to debate the question of whether anyone who doesn't embrace one of the persons of the trinity is saved or not. I am leaving it to you to seek the Lord for this. I will only say, if there is a person of the trinity you are not embracing, please pray about it, ask forgiveness, and reconcile.

2. Breaking Ungodly Soul-Ties

Breaking ungodly soul-ties results in instant deliverance. If you made any ungodly covenants, blood pacts, gang or cult membership vows, or have a co-dependency to any person in your life, including your former spouses, parents, siblings, children, friends, or people you had sexual encounters with in your past, you need to break them and repent from them immediately to be free.

3. Wounded Soul

Praying for healing and restoration over your wounded soul results in deliverance. If you have a broken heart, you have a wounded soul. Many adopted children carry broken hearts and wounded souls, regardless of how wonderful their adoptive family is. There is no perfect family. When they see the flaws of their adoptive parents, the enemy magnifies those shortcomings in their minds, which can have a devastating result.

We all have a soul. Our soul gets hurt and bruised by tragic events, divorce, loss of loved ones, abuse, rape, rejection, or any emotional and even physical hurt, including the sins we have committed. The majority of people try to function and survive in life with wounded souls. That is an open door to the enemy. Pray to Jesus and *receive* healing by faith for your soul to be healed and restored to wholeness.

Psalm 23 states that the great Shepherd "restores our soul."

4. Removing Generational Curses

When you go to a doctor's office, you are required to fill out forms asking about your parents' or even your grandparents' health history. Just as we inherit our DNA, genes, and chromosomes from our ancestors, in the same way we can also inherit curses and demonic powers and influences from them as a result of their sins.

I have seen people instantly delivered and physically healed when we prayed and removed the generational curses from them. You need to repent from the sins of your families, even though you may not have committed them.

Including me, many people I know repented from their father's or grandfather's sins of gambling, and financial curses were removed and instant blessings started flowing.

I repented and renounced the spirit of Ishmael, long after I came to Christ, because no one told me about it. Right after I repented and renounced it, my heart and attitude changed, and I no longer had the habit of certain behaviors.

5. Forgiveness

I also have seen numerous times when people were delivered just through forgiving others and themselves, without any further step-by-step deliverance prayers. With forgiveness and removal of bitterness and resentment, physical healing takes place as well. Forgiveness is not optional for a person to be set free. It is a *must* if you want to live and walk in the freedom of Christ.

6. Declaring and Praying the Word

The Word of God is a powerful weapon against the devil. If anyone continuously soaks in, dwells in, meditates on, and proclaims the Word of God, the enemy cannot stay in that person's presence.

7. Praise and Worship

Whenever David played his instrument, the demon of torment left Saul. When there is true praise and worship (not a platform business, but a sincere exaltation and glorification of God) demonic powers cannot stay. They will leave instantly. They get tormented as you praise and worship.

8. Reconciling with and Honoring Your Parents

I have seen instant deliverances that also brought healing and prosperity when individuals reconciled with their parents and began honoring them. The Bible is very clear about honoring the parents. Exodus 20:12 comes with a promise:

> *Honor your father and your mother, so that you may live long*
> *in the land the Lord your God is giving you.*

You may have been abandoned by your parents. I have ministered to many orphans and children who were abandoned or rejected by one or both parents. There were people whose mothers were prostitutes and whose fathers were drug dealers. I have met women raped by their own fathers. Now you may ask—how can you forgive and honor such individuals? Honor doesn't mean you have to be in a close relationship with parents who violated their parental responsibilities, and forgiveness doesn't mean you have to include them in your life or live with them. You can honor your parents by not disrespecting them and not speaking ill of them. If you have truly forgiven the parent who hurt you, you can even give your testimony and share what has happened without bashing them.

Your parents may not be alive and you may have had a very rough relationship with them. You need to pray and release all your feelings, disappointments, and hurts to them and to the Lord.

I have had people praying in tears and sobbing, telling their deceased parents how much they hurt them, neglected them, or abused them, and they said, "I forgive you for abandoning me or abusing me, and now I release all my hurts to Jesus. In my thoughts and speech, I will be honoring my parents."

If you are feeling stuck in your life or are having numerous accidents or failures in business, work, and/or relationships, you need to ask yourself if there are any open doors to the enemy in your life that allow him to steal from you because you've been dishonoring your parents.

If they are alive and didn't physically or sexually abuse you or threaten your life, you may prayerfully consider going to them and making it right with them, regardless of who they are or were.

I know children who haven't talked to their parents for years and would not even allow them to see their grandchildren. I don't want to pronounce any judgments or curses on them without knowing the details of the relationship, but I can tell you that if this type of action is not led by the Holy Spirit, the consequences can be devastating. Many estranged families justify their actions by putting all the responsibility on the Holy Spirit.

If the Holy Spirit does make it clear that you must not have contact with someone—whether for your own protection or your children's, for example—bear in mind that He will never lead you to dishonor your parent. Even if you must draw a line and keep distance, if the Holy Spirit is behind it you will be able to do it honorably, and you will have peace in your spirit. The relationship will not be a "sore spot" for you. If someone bringing up this relationship causes you to get upset or offended or begin to meditate on negative things, take this decision back to God in prayer. There may still be a need for repentance and forgiveness.

Powerful Tips

* *Rejection causes a very serious injury to the soul. Why? It directly attacks our self-worth.*

* *Many children whose parents were divorced, or who were abandoned by their parents, believe in a lie that it was their fault.*

* *People who were raped and molested carry the guilt and shame as if it was their fault until they are set free.*

* *For complete deliverance, soul wounds have to be healed and the person has to choose the truth versus the lies of the devil to be free.*

A SUMMARY *of* DELIVERANCE RULES

R ule #1: Don't give any platform to the enemy, whether in your church or at any of your events. The devil loves attention.

Rule #2: Bind and cast out the spirit of lies and deception.

Rule #3: You can't exercise authority against a possessed person's will. They will be delivered if they want and believe they'll be delivered. You can't convince them.

Rule #4: Only desperate people can get deliverance. You can't want deliverance for them. If the possessed person is passive and not taking the initiative to be delivered, they will most likely get their demons back seven times worse.

Rule #5: Do not be impressed with or afraid of any violent manifestation. Manifestations are signs that the enemy is tormented and bothered by the truth being preached, and the presence of God is aggravating them.

Rule #6: Don't let people who don't know what they are doing pray over the possessed. Praying instead of expelling is just patting the devil on the shoulder. It can backfire.

Rule #7: Use your authority in Christ to first bind the demons, then cast them out. Stand on the Word of God by declaring it. Always prepare the atmosphere before any event for deliverance by exalting the Name of

Jesus and declaring and proclaiming His Word. Magnify Jesus and the power of the blood of Jesus Christ over and over again and again.

Rule #8: Exalt the Name of Jesus and plead the blood of Jesus Christ. Take your lawful spiritual position when engaging the enemy.

Rule #9: Don't give any room to fear. The devil can smell your fear and attack you. Cast out the spirit of fear before any deliverance.

Rule #10: The enemy knows the weaknesses and hindrances in your life. You need to be right with God before performing any deliverance. Repent from all your sins, naming them as the Holy Spirit brings them to your heart one by one, and ask for the cleansing power of the blood of Jesus.

Rule #11: Seek discernment in each and every case. "Holy Spirit, Spirit of Truth, please reveal to me right now what's going on, and what I am dealing with here. I need Your guidance and help in Jesus Christ's Name. Amen."

Rule #12: Remember that no devils are too powerful for you to cast out as long as the possessed person is desperate and willing.

Rule #13: The demonic manifestation can be an attack directed at you, your family, or your church. You need divine wisdom before spending hours on a person. Know when to walk away without allowing the demons to attack you with the torment of failure, and always ask for the cleansing power of the blood of Jesus afterward.

Rule #14: Do not allow children, pregnant women, unbelievers, or people who are in rebellion to be around the possessed person or to lay hands on him or her.

Rule #15: Usually demons possess or oppress people in gangs or groups. You need to identify the leader of the gang to cast all of them out.

Rule #16: You will know a person is completely free when they can freely and joyfully praise and worship Jesus.

Rule #17: After every deliverance you must do a cleansing prayer over yourself, your team, your family, and/or your church.

> *Dear Lord Jesus, I pray the cleansing power of your blood over myself, my family, church, and friends. I declare that I'm a child of God. I'm a child of light and no spirit of darkness can dwell in me or around me. I expel every demonic presence in Your Name, Lord Jesus. I put a blood line of Jesus Christ between the enemy and me, my household, and my church, in Your powerful and matchless Name, Jesus. Amen.*

ABOUT IŞIK ABLA

ŞIK ABLA (pronounced Ishyk) was born in Istanbul, Turkey. She was raised—and verbally and physically abused—in a Muslim home, only to escape into even more severe abuse by the Muslim man she married.

Işık entered college when she was just sixteen, earning a bachelor's degree in literature followed by an advanced business degree. She worked in high-ranking executive positions for some of the largest corporations in Turkey and traveled throughout Europe.

In 1996 she fled to America from her violent Muslim husband after he tried to kill her. After years of struggling to start her career over again in a foreign country and failing in many areas of her personal life, Işık fell into a deep depression and became suicidal.

On the day she was planning to end her life, she had a personal encounter with God. That day, she surrendered her life to Jesus and received the supernatural healing and redemption of Jesus Christ. From that moment on, her life changed miraculously for the better.

After receiving the Lord's call to full-time ministry, she attended Ambassador's Commission School of Ministry, and soon after graduation became an ordained minister. She studied for a Masters in Divinity and attended both Yale and Harvard Universities for further leadership training and courses.

In 2009, Işik began hosting a satellite TV program, which generated an overwhelming public response. Two years later, she began a live call-in program, simulcast on Turkish and Farsi TV channels throughout the Middle East and Europe. The responses started multiplying as the lives of Muslims were being transformed.

Today, Işik's programs are broadcast in 160 countries, on five continents, and in five languages—Turkish, Arabic, Farsi, Urdu, and English—reaching an audience of more than 750 million viewers and engaging more than six million followers through social media. On Facebook alone, she has millions of followers.

In 2016, she focused on social media engagements, hosting weekly Facebook Live videos called *Dream Church*. She was awarded the National Religious Broadcaster's International Impact award for demonstrating a strong personal commitment to proclaiming Christ through electronic media and working with integrity and faithfulness to influence a culture for Christ.

Her message of hope, love, and redemption, found only in a loving God, resonates and continues to reach the Muslim world for Christ. As a Muslim-background believer, she is uniquely poised, knowing the culture, language, and social norms, to authentically and relationally share the good news of Jesus Christ with Muslims.

God's Dream Church is where all people, all nations, all tribes, all colors and cultures are welcomed. People started joining her at every service, from Afghanistan, Iraq, Egypt, United States, Pakistan, England, Kenya, Malaysia, Singapore, Ethiopia, Lebanon, Turkey, Australia, New Zealand, and more.

Praise reports continue to be received from people all over the world who are part of Dream Church.

Radio Programs

- Began airing Embracing New Life revival messages on radio networks.
- Işık's Turkish radio program, titled "Ask IŞIK," airs in Turkey and beyond multiple times daily.

Songs

Işık and her husband wrote and composed the songs "I Just Said Yes" and "He'll Never Leave You." They have also written other songs that are being translated into multiple languages.

Notes